Moneylove 3.0 Vol 2

New Digital Age Sequel

From

A Pioneering Prosperity Teacher

by

Jerry Gillies

Edited by Tony Busse

ALSO BY JERRY GILLIES

MONEYLOVE: How to Get the Money You Deserve for Whatever You Want

MEN ON WOMEN: 101 men Reveal Their deepest desires, Feelings and Fears

PSYCHOLOGICAL IMMORTALITY: Using Your Mind to Extend Your Life

TRANSCENDENTAL SEX: A Meditative Approach to Increasing Sexual Pleasure

FRIENDS: The Power and Potential of the Company You Keep

MY NEEDS, YOUR NEEDS, OUR NEEDS: A Handbooks For Discovering Each Other and Enhancing Your Love Potential

ISBN: 978-1-7346006-0-5

Editor's Note: (Beginning)

Editor's Note: *Moneylove 3.0 was originally published in digital format. It is so jammed-packed with vital information and contains such a large amount of incredible content that each of the 12 Chapters could easily be books on their own. As a result, a print edition of this work would come in at over 700 pages! - too cumbersome for many reasons. As a result, we have elected to break it up into 3 Volumes that will each include the Introduction and several Chapters.*

Welcome to Volume 2 which will cover Chapters 6-9, the Instruction Manual for the Book, the Introduction and the Additional Resources Section of the Original work. This is a book unlike any you've read before and we strongly encourage you to follow Jerry's instructions on how to use the book and to heed his call to "Do the Damn Exercises!". It is our great hope that the ideas and exercises contained in these books will fill you with "Robust Expectations" and lead you to the "Joyful and Triumphant" results the author intended.

This book is dedicated to six good friends and mentors who would definitely have been a part of it if they were still around. Wait, they are still around in spirit and actually are a part of it.

Ray Bradbury

Leo Buscaglia

Norman Cousins

Ken Keyes, Jr.

Og Mandino

Ric Masten

Hip Hip Hooray!
My Acknowledgments

I know it's usual for an author to state he or she couldn't have written their book without the support and assistance of a sometimes long list of people. Not true in my case! I definitely could have written this without any help at all. Of course, it would have then been a very short and not nearly as good a book--but it could've been done.

One of the things I am most proud of in my life, and a way in which I have definitely left a major thumbprint on the world, is my excellent taste in choosing teachers and mentors and friends and colleagues. I have been so blessed with so many supporters and fantastic contributors to this work. Yes, Moneylove 3.0 might have still been written without the support of Rupa Cousins, Barry Dunlop, Christina Makrides, Leo Quinn, and Mary Ann Somervill--but not nearly as well or nearly as soon. My list of contributors, whom I also call faculty members, and whose wisdom added vast value and profound dimensions to this volume, I will list alphabetically:

Martin Boroson, Tony Busse, Marianne Cantwell, Rupa Cousins, Stephanie Donegan, Michael Dunlop, Barry Dunlop, David Friedman, Edwene Gaines, Allen Klein, Christina Makrides, Sonia Milton, Rickie Moore, Maria Nemeth, Joe Nuckols, Leo Quinn, SQuire Rushnell, Christine Segal, Nicholas Tart, Marta Vago, Maggy Whitehouse, Barbara Winter.

I did not include their titles and the many books they've written, since I elaborate on all of that in the segments or Books in which their contributions appear in the upcoming pages. Along with Internet links for most of them to find out more about them. To everyone involved in this transformative creation, my deeply felt gratitude and reverence. In one of the many ways Moneylove 3.0 is different than other books, when I look over that list, I see not only contributors, and distinguished collaborators, but new and old friends, and it is a heartwarming experience indeed to know how much they gave of themselves and their wisdom to make this a unique and highly conscious effort.

Volume 2: Books 6 through 9 of Moneylove 3.0

CONTENTS

Instruction Manual for Moneylove 3.0

"Everyone is flailing through this life without an owner's manual, with whatever modicum of grace and good humor we can manage."

Anne Lamott

Yes, you've got it right, this is your Instruction Manual for **Moneylove 3.0.** It's part of my quest to make this the most powerful learning tool it can be, as well as the most unique book ever produced. And I certainly don't want any readers flailing through it.

Of course, if you're like me, you'll immediately put it away and go right to the heart of the matter, starting with the Introduction. I cannot count the number of instruction manuals I have ignored. You'd think this ignoring would be the last thing, and least sensible thing I would do, considering how technologically-challenged I am. Even my high tech electric toothbrush and toaster give me problems from time to time. That's when I go to the instruction manual, and it's often too late then.

So maybe instead of an instruction manual, I should call this a learning aid, or an explanation of how to get more out of what I have written. No, I think I'll stick with Instruction Manual and leave you to your own devices in terms of how seriously you consider reading it or discarding it. **Moneylove 3.0** will definitely work amazingly well without it. But I can also safely say that those who put the time and energy in to read it and actually put some of the strategies I suggest into practice, will notice more immediate and more satisfying results.

And because I wouldn't ask you to do anything I wouldn't do--I just bought a high tech USB microphone (whatever that is) and I am going to read the instruction manual word for word.

A Sign of My Respect for You

I am <u>not</u> writing what I believe is a first, an Instruction Manual for a book, because I think you are so stupid you need one to get through it all.

This is not an act of condescension, but a way I have of demonstrating my appreciation and respect for you. I am assuming you are the kind of person who has always read my books, my blog, listened to my audios, or attended my workshops--a smart, self-aware, and self-appreciating human being on a positive path forward in his or her life.

My intention was really to give some guidelines to those who are capable of making it much <u>more</u> than a book. I think there is more in this manual to do with where you go with all this <u>information</u> and <u>knowledge</u> and <u>wisdom</u> (three separate and distinct things as I am sure you know) to turn it into a continuing training, teaching, and inspirational source in your life after your first read-through. While I also know you are more self-motivating than most people out there, I still wanted to provide you with some tools to put into action, because I know you are the kind of person who wants to get every last drop of usefulness out of this, much as the Eskimo uses every tiny part of the whale to improve his life.

A Quite Different Book

One of the first things you will notice as you read **Moneylove 3.0** is that it <u>is</u> quite different from most books, perhaps all books, in several notable ways. For one thing, I have largely left unedited the comments from my contributors or interview subjects. I refuse to pander to short attention spans. Also, I felt it useful for you, as a reader, to get a sense of who was delivering these gems of wisdom and practical suggestions. I trust you are fully capable of finding them all, and you might even note the parts you find especially motivating, inspiring, or useful in a practical way. Too many so-called self-help books don't allow the reader to self-help at all, they strain and dilute and predigest the information like so much psychological or intellectual baby food. Also, if I did heavy editing, I might just cut out something someone said that would be very significant for you.

A Clear Vision

I have a very clear vision of what I want to achieve and it's an ambitious one. I want you to immediately start using some of the suggestions to change every aspect of your life for the better. It's certainly not all about or just about money, though I would love to see you get rich. If you work at it and thus it works for you, then I cannot help but benefit. And I hope you have a clear vision of what you want to achieve.

I don't mean to insult you or myself, but we have not been keeping up. **Moneylove 3.0** is about how to become more prosperous in a rapidly changing economy and happier in a rapidly changing world. presenting timeless principles in a new way to help you succeed in one of the most transformational periods in human history. Almost nothing is as we knew it ten or twenty years ago, and it would be impossible for any human being to have kept up with all the changes. Things have been moving so rapidly in technology, science, the economy, global relationships, and even social interaction that few people have had the time to step back, go inward, and reflect on exactly what the hell is happening--to the world, their work, and the people they once knew and loved.

My Contributors are Actually a Prosperity Faculty

One of the biggest ways in which this is a unique creation is in that I invited some of the authors, teachers, coaches, and mentors I most admire and have learned from to make major contributions in sharing their own thoughts and ideas on my subject. You will notice that their segments are sometimes unusually long. That's because I wanted you to be able to get as much of their good stuff as possible. For most of them, I have included a live link, a way you can just click on their website for more of what they offer.

There is enough information in Moneylove 3.0 to get you moving in the right direction. Human growth, elevation, enlightenment, and getting on the right path with passion and purpose, is a lifelong process. It's also a process that can be fun, exciting, filled with promise and conscious results. But the best way to do it is one step at a time, and many gifted teachers and coaches suggest those be baby steps.

Here is one way to go with all this that I think will be very effective:

1. **Read this entire volume.** By all means, when you enjoy a passage by one of my contributors, take a look at their website.

2. **Do the exercises and processes as you go along.** In addition to interviewing her extensively on her amazing grasp of the world of the Internet, I have borrowed and repeat frequently, Marianne Cantwell's admonition from her book, **How To Be A Free Range Human**, where she says: **Do the damn exercises!**

3. Read it aloud, taking your time. This is a powerful way to increase the power of any book you read offering new ideas about anything. It accesses a part of your brain that may not be reached by mere silent reading. Though you are welcome to find the best way to put this into practice, I suggest reading **Moneylove 3.0** all the way through first, then going back and reading one chapter/book at a time out loud. You can do this alone, but if you know someone, a friend or loved one, you think would appreciate a particular section, read it to them. You can even do this with distant friends via Skype or FaceTime. Or, you can record your reading it out loud and create your own audio book.

On to The Graduate School of Getting More Involved

And here are a few more suggestions I would call my graduate school program for those who have already finished reading all of **Moneylove 3.0**, and would like to make it more an individual experience.

1. Go to a fairly long book, like **TimeLove**, and edit it and rewrite it so that it is more to your liking, and keeps the points you think are most important. This will help you absorb more of the important ideas it contains, as well as giving you the experience that you are in charge of the information you take in. Being able to copy and paste this PDF digital book makes that a lot easier.

2. Get a few of your friends or colleagues together and tell them several important ideas you've read and really like. You can make this a discussion group, and see if they can see the same useful ideas you chose work-

ing for them. I like Sonya Milton's statement, "I teach so that I can know."

3. Write a two-part essay on, "What is Right about **Moneylove 3.0** and What Can Be Improved in Future Editions?" It would be highly unlikely that we exactly agree on every idea and point I've written or elicited from my contributors. The more you can make this your own creative venture, in terms of your individual desires and comfort level, the better it will work for you.

4. When you feel you have actually gotten desired results from putting at least one of my ideas into action, write and tell me about it. Obviously, I like getting emails of this sort, but it also will allow you to crystalize what value you received, and perhaps give you some thoughts on how to get even more for yourself from this work.

5. Each week for the next year, pick one sentence from one segment that will serve as your prosperity mantra for that week. It should be a sentence that speaks to you, that motivates or inspirits you. You can decide to post it on your wall, or add it to your computer's desktop, and to write it out or read it out loud as many times as you think will work best for you. But mostly, this is the sentence you will see as your mission statement for this particular week.

These exercises are not gimmicks, but rather ways you can make **Moneylove 3.0** a more dynamic and powerful tool in your psychological arsenal. Give any or all of them a chance, and you will be amazed at how much more profoundly you will begin seeing changes in your results.

The sum, combined total of everything offered on the following pages, contains ideas and revelations that may surprise or even shock you. I do not come from a position that I am richer or smarter than you.

But I can pretty well declare that I've spent more time studying and learning this stuff than you have, and I have been unusually fortunate to attract teachers and mentors, some famous and some not, who have been the cream of the crop in terms of wisdom and coming up with practical solutions and inspiring ideas for living a life of true abundance and joy.

I've attempted to make this experience circular and permanent rather than linear and temporary. That is, I am laying down certain rules, principles, and ideas about prosperity that you can keep dipping into as you keep moving forward and upward in your life.

This is designed to be more simply functional than the way much information is presented today, zipping past our perceptions and cerebral cortexes faster than we can take it all in, and then disappearing as its forced out by the next new shiny thing.

This approach reflects my assertion that one of the new skills we all need moving forward in this new millennium (and so much has been happening so fast we sometimes forget it is a new millennium), one of the primary skills we all need to develop and keep honing is that of discernment, that of creating an inner editor to let the useful stuff in and keep the information overwhelm at bay. The new process about doing that inner editing, I call **The Law of Subtraction**, is presented in Book Three. It is a practical way to deal with what I have termed Information Asphyxiation.

I have talked a lot about this being unique in many different ways. One of those ways is that it is not meant to be at its most effective by the reader starting at page one and going through to the end, whether that takes days or weeks. For many people that would be a good idea, but if you are one of those readers, you should know that you are cheating yourself if that is it, if you just read it once cover to cover, and then put it aside.

This is an experience more than it is a book. The good thing about that is that it has no deadline, you don't have to return it to the library, you are not racing to prepare for a test. I'm sure as you looked over the table of contents, you saw some subjects that most interested you. This is not a volume for masochists, you don't have to punish yourself by reading stuff that isn't speaking to you right now just to get a few pages further along, you can go right to that section. So, again, if Time is your big issue, definitely read Book Five, **TimeLove** and its Appendix right away, before anything else (except perhaps this Instruction Manual and the Introduction--but even these are not mandatory).

One part of this volume, in particular, is not designed to be read all the way through all at once, and that is Book Eleven, **QuoteLove**. Even if you are overly ambitious, if you wanted to apply all 100 Quotercises to each of the 100 included quotes in turn, it could take months and miss the point of my approach to living. Take it nice and easy, don't stress or punish yourself. The section or Book is a resource, as many of the sections are, meant to be revisited time and again. It might be fun to take maybe five of the Quotercises and try them out. And if you find it a worthwhile and rewarding process, look forward to going back on a regular basis. This is a learning program, but you set your own schedule and your own choices. There's a lot here, and I don't want to regret including so much because some folks overdose and need medical care.

This all will work best for you if you begin it as an adventure, do the damn exercises, and have as much fun as you possibly can in the process.

Book Six: Carpe Serendipity

Most people have had a taste of serendipity in their lives. Some consider these converging apparent coincidences as happy accidents, some consider them messages from God, others feel they happen when your life is in alignment and you are on the right path. Many call them lucky. But I don't really choose to label them, just to experience them, when they occur, as productively as possible.

Seize Them With Gusto

I titled this book, not just to be cute or clever, but to suggest that these are events that are meant to be taken advantage of in our lives, to be seized with gusto. Every serendipitous event in my life, and there have been many, has had a much more profound payoff potential than I may have realized at the time. And each time I was alert and aware enough to make the most of these happy coincidences or accidents or divine messages, I have benefited greatly.

I'll give you an example of one that happened just weeks before starting to write this book. My following up and taking advantage of the circumstances and the awareness's they produced has added another wise and very prosperity conscious contributor to the book.

Amazing Serendipity Spanning 50 Years

Before beginning work on this book, in the Fall of 2014, I was preparing my bestselling 1978 book, **Moneylove**, for digital publication. I wanted to check the book for any typographical or grammatical errors, and also see whether the material all held up as well as I and many others thought it did. I was pleasantly surprised to find a number of ideas and anecdotes that I had forgotten completely, including this segment which appeared in perhaps my favorite chapter, *"Worklove"*. I was talking about the value of sharing yourself and your ideas:

> *"The more someone is willing to help others prosper, the more prosperous he or she will become. Every time I've shared a valuable idea, it's come back to me a hundredfold. During my early days in broadcasting, I was more fortunate than many colleagues and became quite successful at a very young age. I always went out of my way to answer questions and offer advice to those men and women who wanted to find out how to get into radio or television, or those who wanted to advance faster than they were advancing. I always waited to be asked, however, since I have a certain bias against unasked-for-advice givers. (Though maybe all of us self-help book authors fit into just that category!)*

> *Anyway, some of those young men and women I helped get into broadcasting, or get ahead, are now top management people or nationally known performers. I've never asked for anything in return, but it's a nice feeling to know I would probably never have any trouble returning to that field if I so desired, and that I'd have friends and supporters in positions where they could advise or assist me. (I have no plans to return to broadcasting, but my friends in the industry do come in very handy when I go out promoting a book on talk shows across the country.)"*

As I was reading this, I thought about Joe Nuckols. He had been a college freshman in Richmond, Virginia, who started working part-time at WRVA Radio in 1964, where I was a top-rated newsman. He was an enthusiastic 18-year-old, who had always wanted to work in radio and had done various stints at other stations. He would come in during the evening hours and do a lot of practicing. I would often offer suggestions, acting as a sort of mentor, playing the wise elder at the age of twenty-four!

After leaving WRVA, first to work at KYW Newsradio in my hometown, Philadelphia, then to go on to New York, I didn't think about Joe. It wasn't until twenty-five years later, in 1989 that his name came up again.

A friend was organizing a Moneylove Seminar for me in Ft. Lauderdale. As part of promoting it, she contacted local media to arrange interviews, and was particularly interested in getting me on a new all-motivational radio station, WNN, in Pompano Beach. She told me, excitedly, "Jerry, I talked to the owner/manager of the station and he says he knows you. His name is Joe Nuckols!"

It was great seeing Joe again, and meeting his wife Terry. He had made an arrangement with Nightingale-Conant to play segments from their motivational and inspirational tapes on the air, and called their effort The Winners News Network. He told me the Moneylove tape album was just about the most popular and most requested. He really promoted my seminar and it was a big success. There were moments, after I left Florida, moreover, when I thought the all-motivational radio idea was a great one and wondered whether I should see if I could get involved in it, but I never pursued it.

Zoom Ahead Again

Zoom ahead another twenty-five years and I did something after reading that passage in **Moneylove** and remembering Joe Nuckols that I couldn't have done before the Internet. I Googled Joe. Another great thing about the Internet is that when I say I "Googled", you can duplicate my actions immediately and see for yourself what I discovered. What I found was that Joe went on to be very very successful in broadcasting and kept up his relationship with Nightingale-Conant.

Joe was now running the company's weekly podcast, and had written, narrated, and produced their first feature-length film, *The DARE Matrix*, which is actually four motivational films. In addition, Joe has written a novel about a motivational speaker, **When Angels Lie** (which will be a series), and a motivational book, **It Is No Secret**: *Release Your Prosperity Potential from Your Past, Present, and Possibilities*. Joe is also considered a major figure in personal development.

Can you see why I decided I wanted to get in touch with Joe? Again, with the help of the Internet and social media, I was able to very easily do so. I simply looked him up on Facebook and sent him a message saying I would like to interview him for this book. He responded quickly with:

"Hey Jerry, What a great pleasure to hear from you. It would be an honor to be interviewed. Feel free to email me to set up a time."

The Serendipity Goes On

And so, I got some great ideas from Joe for this work. But that's only one part of my serendipity story. The very next Sunday, I noticed that CBS Sunday Morning was featuring a segment on coincidences. Well, I had to watch that after this big coincidence had just happened. And who was one of the main people they interviewed? None other than SQuire Rushnell (yes, he does spell it that way).

SQuire is actually the very man who hired me away from WRVA where I met Joe Nuckols so many years ago! He was an executive at KYW Newsradio in Philadelphia. He had heard me on the air as he was driving around, and liked me enough to make me an offer I couldn't refuse. SQuire is also now an inspirational speaker and creator of the term Godwinks and author of a series of bestselling Godwinks books. According to SQuire, a Godwink is: *"An event or personal experience, often identified as coincidence, so astonishing that it could only have come from divine origin."* This sure sounded like serendipity to me.

SQuire also was a major figure in broadcasting after he left Philadelphia, and produced such shows as Good Morning America and School House Rock.

Of course, I went to Facebook and messaged him, too, and he said he remembered me well and would be happy to do an interview.

I don't know whether any of these amazing coincidences were just that, a divine message, or a happy accident--one of the definitions of serendipity, but I definitely will be following up on both connections.

Seize Your Serendipity Opportunities

I titled this, *Carpe Serendipity.* for a specific reason. As I said, most of us have had sequences of events like this in our lives, and what I am suggesting is that, as is certainly true for me, we often miss out on opportunities they present.

Playing Your Luck

A lot of people would also describe these converging events as good luck. I talked about the concept of Playing Your Luck in the Moneylove Manifesto. The concept came from John Kluge, who was the richest man in America, according to Forbes, in the 1980s. Coincidently (or luckily, or serendipitously, or God-winkingly), I once worked for Kluge, though I never met him, when I was a newsman at WNEW in New York, the flagship station of his Metromedia media empire.

How Serendipity Produced The Richest Man in America

John Kluge loved to tell the story of how he was walking on a street in Washington, D.C. at a time when he was considering his next move in business. He ran into a young man he had known some years before, who told him the old Dumont Broadcasting Network was for sale. Kluge ended up buying it and it became the Metromedia broadcasting empire, which he sold in 1986 for two billion dollars. He would emphasize that meeting that young man on the street was lucky, but what mattered was how he parleyed that luck into a fortune by taking action to buy the network.

What Poker Can Teach You

John Kluge was also a famous poker player and earned his way through college with his card-playing skills. That's where he learned an important rule that I also learned as a successful poker player. It *is* a matter of luck, but not in terms of waiting for lucky cards to come your way.

In life, as in poker you have good luck and bad luck, and it's how you play your luck that matters, whichever is happening. I have noticed that bad players tend to raise their stakes when they are losing, and often put away some money when they are winning. The successful players, on the other hand, know that when you're winning is the time to go all in, and when you're losing is the time to slow down and maybe even quit the game for a while. In fact, there was quite an uproar when John Kluge was quoted in Forbes as saying:

> If you want your kid to succeed in business, maybe you shouldn't send him or her to business school. Teach him to play cards, instead. Card playing teaches you that luck is important, but how you play your luck is even more important."

No, Not That Bill and Hillary

On that same CBS Sunday Morning segment where I saw SQuire Rushnell, they began the feature with the wonderful story of Bill and Hillary Solomon.

Bill Solomon says, *"There were just too many coincidences for it to be random."*

It started four decades earlier when Bill's mother and Hillary's father were high school friends. They hadn't been in touch with each other for those forty years.

Hillary continues the story, *"They met by chance and realized that one had a son named Bill and the other had a daughter named Hillary. And guess who was in the White House when they reconnected?"*

The two high school friends then discovered that their daughter and son both lived in New York and said, *"We've got to fix them up."* Still another amazing coincidence: in a city of 7 million, Bill and Hillary lived in the same neighborhood on the same street and in the same building! Hillary in an 11th-floor apartment filled with funky flea market finds, and Bill seven floors directly below and in line with her place on the fourth floor in a bachelor pad with lots of stereo equipment and a poster of Marilyn Monroe. Somehow the two had never noticed each other. When they heard about the matchmaking scheme, both cringed.

Bill's Happy Fate Was Sealed

Bill didn't need too many more coincidences to get the idea that this was meant to happen. He met a female co-worker in his apartment building lobby. He asked what she was doing there, and she said *"I have a really good friend who lives in your building."*--and, of course, it was Hillary. At that, Bill said to his friend, *"Oh my God, I have her number in my pocket."* So he made the call and they got married two years later, in 1998.

SQuire Rushnell and Godwinks

SQuire Rushnell, my old boss, likes to remind people that John Adams and Thomas Jefferson, who both signed the Declaration of Independence and were both Presidents, both died exactly on July 4th,1826 the 50th anniversary of the signing. SQuire says, *"That's what started me questioning whether there was something more to coincidence that just coincidence."*

Of course, this same coincidence was coincidently mentioned in Book Two, Robust Expectations, as an example of how people may live beyond their expected time if some important event is scheduled. I imagine the 50th Anniversary of the Fourth of July was pretty significant to Adams and Jefferson.

Squire's Description of Godwinks

He describes what he calls Godwinks as:

One of those little coincidences that make you say one of two things, "Wow, what are the odds of that?" or: "I wonder if that coincidence is evidence of divine origin." Yes, Godwinks are like gifts left on the doorstep, and my job in talking and writing about this is to get you to open the door and then open your gift.

Scientists Try to Ruin the Fun of Serendipity

Scientists scoff and say coincidences, Godwinks, and serendipity, are all just co-occurrences of random chance. On the other hand, some research indicates that having a feeling that they are a part of your life can have strong positive effects on your outlook on life

I'll ignore many of the scientists who seem fascinated by coincidences and then try to create theories to fit the facts, though I am amused by one such explanation called The Law of Truly Large Numbers. The mathematicians who developed this silly idea say that if you have a large enough sample of events, any outrageous thing, including an amazing coincidence, is likely to happen. Maybe you have to be a mathematician to grasp that as a serious effort. As SQuire Rushnell says, *"Mathematicians will always have an answer for anything. I put more faith in the grand designer than I do in accidents happening numerically."*

Serendipity As a Sign of Alignment

Some of my spiritual and metaphysical friends tell me that when serendipitous events occur it means you are on the right path in life, you are living your true purpose, or you are in alignment with your destiny.

In his book, **Divine Alignment**: *How Godwink Moments Guide Your Journey*, SQuire Rushnell says,

> *Only when you stop and open your mind to the Divine Alignment possibilities do you see the marvelous connections and invisible threads that connect you from one person to another. You begin to understand that your life is not an accident at all. You're not like a twig randomly floating down a stream to destinations unknown. Right from birth, we come equipped with a highly sophisticated navigational package that--through an internal voice of intuition and godwinks--divinely aligns us with people, as well as events, who assist us in reaching our destiny and keep us from losing our way."*

Now, I have read a lot of books on spiritual approaches and explanations, but I must admit SQuire's has a special quality I like, even though I am not as much a person of faith as he seems to be. I especially like this statement he makes:

> *As you travel through life, your hands are on the steering wheel most of the way. And one of the gifts you are given, factory installed, is free will. You're free to go too fast or too slow. To be reckless or responsible. Or even free to drive off the highway altogether, if that's what you choose. You*

also have the free will to acknowledge--or to ignore--that you are not here by accident."

I can see where accepting this belief and that you are in this great place right now would allow more serendipity to show up.

Joe Nuckols

The first star of my opening serendipity story is Joe Nuckols, and he had an interesting approach that goes beyond serendipity into all aspects of having a successful life. Joe has met and talked to and introduced at various conferences, the leading lights of the whole motivational/ inspirational movement, like Zig Ziglar, Brian Tracy, Og Mandino, Denis Waitley, thanks to his connection with Nightingale-Conant, the world's largest producer and distributor of these kinds of personal development audios and videos. Joe not only has written about this in his book, **It is No Secret**: *Release Your Prosperity Potential from Your Past, Present, and Possibilities*, but is also a motivational speaker himself. I like his simple, but effective formula:

Joe's Formula for Success

*"The whole idea of serendipity and directing our lives and falling into line with what our purpose is, for me kind of loops back to the philosophy I wrote about in my book, **It Is No Secret**. It's called D.A.R.E., and when I did these four films for Nightingale-Conant, I expanded it to the D.A.R.E. Matrix.*

The D stands for your Destiny, your Desires, your Dreams. A is for Accurate Thinking. For me, accurate thinking is a lot more important than just positive thinking. You need to think those positive thoughts that, 'I am great,' but you also have to be realistic and have accurate thinking apply.

The R stands for Resources, which is the serendipity of life, the great abundance of resources that are coming to each and every one of us all the time. We all have resources we can tap. Those resources may be in a mentor such as yourself, and the skills that you may develop from that mentor. The resources may be money, may not be money. It may be SQuire Rushnell, who hired you to come to KYW. He was a resource. He heard you, you were ready and he was ready to hire you. The fourth letter, E, is for Execution. Everything else is just conversation unless you actually do something. So you had to get in the car and drive up to Philadelphia from Richmond and take on the job or you wouldn't have made it.

Everybody has to have that sense of urgency to get into action.

This whole D.A.R.E. philosophy is about creating your own serendipity, where you look at what your desires are, your dreams, and the thing that you love, your passion. You think about it accurately. You find and attract the resources that help you execute where you want to go."

It took me fifty years from the time I first met Joe to quoting him in this book. Without the serendipity of coming upon that segment in the 1978 **Moneylove**, remembering and thinking about him and wondering what he was doing now, I would not have discovered this resource, and how much our ideas are in synch. A serendipitous connection like this brings home for me the wonderful things that can flow toward you if you are ready, willing, and able. And they can go way beyond just influencing your life. I definitely think Joe's sharing his D.A.R.E. formula will trigger some positive results for some of you readers, and it all started with a happy accident.

http://www.nightingale.com/authors/joe-nuckols.html

It may also be useful to think of a time when serendipity happened and you didn't recognize it or take advantage of it. Perhaps you were not in an open or receptive mood, or perhaps your life was so full of activity that you didn't have the time or space to notice it.

There are events, I think, in all our lives, where we might say "No" to something we could have said "Yes," to and unleashed a whole bonanza of possibilities. And sometimes we have said, "Yes," when saying "No" would have brought some great serendipitous events into our life. No sense fretting about spilled serendipity--the good news is that there are many, many more such amazing happenings awaiting you.

Untapped Possibilities

I can remember a couple of events like this in my past. Some years ago, a friend of mine told me she met a woman who had just become a top executive in a major New York publishing house, and that somehow my name came up. This woman kept on going on about how much she loved **Moneylove** and a couple of my other books. I could have followed up and maybe even shown her some of my book proposals or talked about some new ideas I had. Surely I missed out on some opportunity there.

It's also interesting to speculate what might have been, or what could have happened if I had kept up with Joe Nuckols. But with this speculation comes another realization. I am very pleased with where I am now in my life, and the creative energy has never flowed more easily. Who knows if this would have happened if I had been willing or ready to follow up on those earlier possibilities?

I just thought of another one. A friend in Los Angeles told me that one of Nora Ephron's co-writers on "Sleepless in Seattle" was a huge fan of **Moneylove**. If I had seized that moment, it might have led to some great serendipity, and maybe I would have even met the late Nora Ephron. I was a big fan of hers.

Moneylove Action Exercise: Serendipity in Your Life

This might be a good time to take a few moments to explore your own experiences of serendipitous events in your life.

1. Can you remember one episode of serendipity that was very impactful?

2. On a scale of 1 to 10, how open and available are you for these occurrences to happen?

3. Can you remember an amazing coincidence that you think you could have taken more advantage of, or enjoyed a lot more?

4. A lot of coincidences have happened on Social Media now that we are so connected. Several friends and relatives I haven't heard from in many years have been in touch through my blog or Facebook. Can you think of one of these that happened for you?

5. One action step you can take that may or may not lead to serendipity is to go to a site such as Facebook, and search for someone you really enjoyed in your life, but whom you haven't seen for at least ten to twenty years. Look them up, message them that you'd like to reconnect, and then let go of any expectations that they'll respond. Prepare to be surprised!

Another Amazing Coincidence

I was talking on Skype with my friend, Tom Weidlein, who

lives in California, and whom I have known since the mid-1990s. He read something on my blog about my having worked for WRVA Radio in Richmond, Virginia, which he hadn't known. He asked if I knew a young guy named Dave Dewitt when I was there. They had been college roommates and have stayed in close touch over the years. I did remember Dave, though I didn't know him as well as I did Joe Nuckols. I knew his wife, Cathy, better, as she was a friend of my girlfriend's. Tom told me that Dave has become one of the world's leading experts on chili peppers and spicy foods, and author of many books on those subjects. Would it be too much to suggest that the fact that I love spicy foods adds to the coincidence?

A Fun Serendipity Experience On a Plane

There's no doubt that once you start remembering coincidences in your life, you be able to access more of them in your memory. I just remembered the one that occurred on a flight to New York. I don't even remember where I was coming from. It was the end of a two week intensive book tour for the paperback edition of **Moneylove**. But I noticed someone reading that paperback edition about four rows in front of me.

I went up to this person, who happened to be a lovely blonde stewardess getting a free ride. I was going to be so cool and ask her how the book was, but I was so excited at seeing someone actually reading it that I blurted out as soon as I approached her seat, "I wrote that. I'm Jerry Gillies, the author!" It sounded as stupid then as it does now. She looked up and figuring it was just some guy trying to hit on her, said, "I don't believe you." I had to show her my driver's license. She then told me that two of the stewardesses (this was before they were known as "flight attendants.") were joining her to go and see and support a friend who was performing in a local night club.

They invited me to join them, and it sounded like great fun, but my girlfriend was picking me up at the airport and we hadn't seen each other in two weeks. To tease me, as I exited the plane they clung to either side of me and acted very affectionate as I walked toward my girlfriend. I had a lot of explaining to do, but it also felt pretty cool. I still, every once in a while, wonder what my joining them at that nightclub would have led to. I don't even remember the performer's name, so she might have gone on to become someone really famous. And I actually met my blonde stewardess again several years later at a National Speakers Association conference. She was now giving motivational talks and we had a good laugh remembering our initial meeting.

Life is filled with all kinds of possibilities, and I imagine we miss a lot of them because we might be preoccupied, or in a mood or state of mind where we are not really looking for good things to happen. Here's my point: Good things are always happening all around us, and we need to make room in our minds to see them and receive them and participate in them.

Being in a poverty consciousness negative mindset doesn't just make the moment a bummer; it may be preventing all sorts of possibilities from benefiting us as time goes forth. It is similar to the sort of destructive lack of consciousness that is possessed by polluters or destroyers of wildlife, who just don't have the vision or humanity to see that the damage they do goes far far beyond what is happening and what they are doing right now.

The Ripple and Butterfly Effects in Humans

A lot of people have accepted the idea of the ripple effect, of small actions having an impact of ever-increasing significance. And we accept the Butterfly Effect, a part of chaos theory that developed the popular metaphor of a butterfly flapping its wings in Africa having an effect in some way in a faraway part of the world.

But very few people see that this can also be true in human consciousness. Ignoring something potentially good for you, or receiving something potentially bad is a human action and reaction that happens with alarming frequency. This is why many miss out on the possibility of serendipity in their lives.

Martin Boroson, in Book Five, **TimeLove**, suggests that we need to create spaciousness in our minds. This is not just an offhanded suggestion that you might or might not see as valuable. It is vitally essential to our emotional, mental, and physical wellbeing.

In the story of Bill and Hillary Solomon and their romantic serendipity, there's an important message. Even though they were busy and almost missed out on their life together, and even though they were busily engaged in the hustle and bustle of the busiest city in the world, they managed to make room in their minds and their lives for something wonderful to happen. And not only did they make room for something to happen, but they made room to make the right decisions and recognize it was happening in the moment.

Is there someone living in your building or neighborhood whom you haven't gotten to know or reached out to, whereby you might be setting a chain of effects and events in motion--even if it is only to make a new friend, or someone who can provide an answer to a challenge that comes up for you?

This is not just about the magic that seems in the air when something serendipitous happens, it is about every possible positive event that could be happening in your life, but hasn't yet manifested.

A Formula for Creating More Serendipity

Here's a simple formula to follow that may help:

Stop making a conscious effort to remember bad things that happened and thinking about bad things that could eventually happen in your life. These are both fantasies, in other words, they're not happening for you or to you in this moment. Get right with your own subconscious and treat it with the respect it deserves without filling it with crap. Realize that a moment in time when you are completely alone with nothing to do is a space created to let something good in, not a time to whine and complain about being lonely.

Meditating for a moment, as Martin Boroson suggests, may work best for you, but also experiencing the good around you, seeing whatever you may not be achieving as just a drop in the bucket compared to what you might achieve when you put your mind to it. And I mean put your mind to it in a very real and timely manner.

Moneylove Action Exercise: Your Assignment

Your homework assignment for *Carpe Serendipity* is simple. Write a list of serendipitous events that have happened in your life. For each one, think and write about what your circumstances were like when it happened, and whether you think you took full advantage of any possibilities it presented to you.

The more you pay attention to serendipitous events in your life, the more you will learn what kinds of circumstances tend to attract them. Figure out what you might need to change to allow more of them to occur in your life.

Whether you consider this woowoo or unlikely magical stuff, or a mathematical anomaly, or a Godwink, or just a happy accident doesn't really matter if you believe it happens and that it could happen to you.

Another Happy Accident

I connected (or reconnected) with Sonya Milton, another contributor to this book in another happy accident. My good friend, Dr. Rachel Harris, was instrumental in my meeting Sonya and attending Unity San Francisco for the five years she was its minister. Her retiring coincided with my leaving to live in Panama. Rachel says Sonya and I met and liked each other in the 1970s in Miami, but neither Sonya nor I could remember the exact circumstances, though we each thought the other looked familiar. I went to Unity SF to meet Sonya, and enjoyed her message and the positive energy of the congregation. Also, I must confess, I fell in love with the opulent gourmet buffet table set up downstairs after the service on Sunday.

I knew I wanted to talk to Sonya about the "Building A Prosperous Spirit" chapter in this book, but when we talked recently our conversation touched on a number of aspects of prosperity. For instance, she shared:

In 1978 I was in a workshop where you were partnered with someone and would tell each other what you needed or wanted. I needed $6000 to complete my training as a Rolfer (a form of bodywork focused on the connective tissue and designed to put the body more in alignment with gravity). I was going all over the place in trying to come up with a solution to producing that $6000. Finally, my partner says to me, "Why don't you ask me for the money?"

So I asked him for the money and he lent me the money. So here I was, frantically looking for an answer, when all I had to do was clearly ask for what I wanted. It was a great lesson for me, with all the mind games I was playing when all I needed to do was "Ask for what I wanted.

Sonya said this kind of thing has happened several times in her life. I responded by saying this is true for me, too. And like most people, I have sometimes tended to forget how easy it was to get something I wanted by just asking the right question of the right person at the right time.

Although, Sonya Milton, wasn't telling me this story as an example of serendipity, a day or two after the interview, I realized that it was, as are many things are we don't label as serendipity or coincidence. For instance, Sonya decided to take that workshop, and she just happened to end up with this man she didn't know, and they just happened to do an exercise where she got to share what was troubling her.

These serendipitous factors all came together in perfect alignment when he asked her, "Why don't you just ask me for the money?" I wonder whether any other partner she could have paired up with would have had the resources or the inclination to meet her need.

Me and Sally Jesse

As I thought about this subject of serendipity, I found a number of episodes that I didn't identify as serendipity when they happened. Look back on your own life and see whether you can find one or more of these.

My connection with famed talk show hostess, Sally Jesse Raphael, is one example of this. She was going through a rough patch with her husband, when Doubleday sent her a copy of my first book, **My Needs, Your Needs, Our Needs**. She shared it with her husband and they tried a number of my suggested communication exercises. They got their act together and she credited my book with "saving my marriage." She had me on her radio show in Miami and we had a lot of fun. Everything I did from then on, she had me promote on her show, even when she moved to big time radio in New York, and eventually began her TV show.

Sally even asked me if I would substitute for her on the station in Miami for one week, as she had to go to Puerto Rico to visit her ailing father. I did the show and enjoyed inviting friends as guests. It was broadcast from a fancy Coral Gables restaurant, and I could have up to six people for a free gourmet lunch each day. It allowed me to repay a lot of hospitality I had received. And it all started because my book arrived in her life at exactly the moment she and her husband needed to work on their relationship.

The only downside to this was that she so loved my first book that she would rave about it for minutes on end when I was appearing on her show to promote a newer book. This even happened after **My Needs, Your Needs, Our Needs** went out of print. But there is no doubt I made quite a chunk of money from books sold by appearing on "The Sally Jesse Raphael Show". Her marriage did fine, too. As of this writing, she and Karl have been wed 52 years.

And my friend Rachel Harris recently reminded me of still another serendipity moment she was involved in. In 1989, when I was in South Florida for the seminar that Joe Nuckols helped me promote, I visited Rachel in her sprawling Coconut Grove home, located in a very woodsy setting. She informed me that she had recently had a visitor. It was none other than Sally Jesse Raphael and her husband, Karl. They had rented the same house some years earlier and asked if they could come in a look around.

Science and Serendipity

Scientists do scoff at the idea of serendipity being more than random coincidence, but they also consider serendipity the act of finding something worthwhile when you started out looking for something completely different. This happens quite often in scientific research, as it did for Alexander Fleming and his discovery of penicillin in mold when he was doing research on the properties of staphylococci in 1928. Fleming declared, "I certainly didn't plan to revolutionize all medicine by discovering the world's first antibiotic, or bacteria killer. But I suppose that was exactly what I did."

Interestingly enough, it wasn't Fleming who finally introduced penicillin to the world. He abandoned penicillin after seeing how difficult it was to isolate the antibiotic from the mold, and that it would be very hard to produce in any great amounts. He believed that it wouldn't last long enough in the human body to effective destroy bacteria. It was Howard Florey and Ernst Boris Chain at the Radcliffe Infirmary in Oxford who took up the research and after Pearl Harbor, they started mass production, so that it saved countless thousands of lives of Allied forces in World War II.

Florey and Chain shared the Nobel Prize with Fleming. So while Fleming is an excellent example of a serendipitous scientific discovery of immense consequence, he was not able to follow through to manifest the full benefits of that discovery until other researchers took it on.

Pek van Andel

Dutch inventor and scientist Pek van Andel has given a master class titled "Serendipity at Work". He first won notice when he developed an artificial cornea, but gained his greatest fame when millions of online viewers watched his video on the MRI scanning of the sex act. He is working on a PhD on the concept of serendipity, which he describes as:

"The gift of making an unsought finding and/or its harvest: an 'accidental' discovery, invention or creation in science, technique or art." van Andel claims to have the largest archive in the world on serendipity, and says that, "In the chaos of these enigma, novelty, and anomaly-triggered serendipities, I found an order of forty patterns."

He tells us that these patterns introduce a new and stimulating perspective on serendipity and he hopes his findings will help people (one presumes mainly fellow scientists) to expect the unexpected and find even what they weren't looking for.

Pek van Andel, despite focusing on the scientific incidence of serendipity, has a thesis that can impact any serendipitous activity in anyone's life. He says, *"To find something really new you can't go logically from the old to the new. You need an unpredictable element, often a surprising observation."* He also says that a really new finding is made by design as well as accident.

Opening More Space for Serendipity

What van Andel 's words mean to us is that people can set

up circumstances in which serendipity is more likely to occur. As I and others suggest in terms of taking charge of your time, you are opening up space in your life for surprises, and some of these may indeed involve serendipity.

I think the serendipity factor also can affect traditional goal setting techniques. Many teachers and authors have stressed the need for single-minded focus on the goals you want to achieve in your life. But if you want to create something really new that will have you leaving a big thumbprint on the world, you must leave room for surprises. You must be open to the very real possibility that you will find something which produces much better results than reaching your original goal.

How Serendipity Led to a New Career for Me

An example of this from my own life: I was working at NBC Radio in New York as a newsman, commentator, and business reporter. I was very interested in psychology, particularly humanistic psychology and the human potential movement based largely on Abraham Maslow's ideas about self-actualized human beings. Because of this interest, I made every effort to do any interviews scheduled with psychologists and psychiatrists. I also proposed and got approval for a documentary series called, "Growing and Groping In Groups". I got to explore a lot of these groups which were happening in New York, some led by visiting faculty from Esalen Institute in Big Sur, California, and some at the New York centers, Aureon Institute, and Anthos Institute.

The director of Aureon Institute was a well-known psychologist, Dr. Harold Streitfeld, who had written a bestselling compilation of many exercises and games used in workshops and encounter groups, called **Growth Games**. I interviewed Harold Streitfeld extensively and attended several of his encounter groups and large lighthearted workshops.

At some point, Harold suggested that I might make a good workshop leader. Here's where the serendipity came in. I had never considered such a thing, had never done it, and in fact had entered radio because it was a good way to be creative and not have to interact with lots of people face-to-face. I was still carrying around the remnants of a very shy childhood.

But Harold was insistent that he saw something in me that I didn't see. He offered to schedule a workshop and co-lead it with me. It was a scary proposition, but despite my shyness, I was always adventurous and unwilling to let new opportunities pass me by. I agreed, and we decided to create a workshop of communication games so men and women could get to know each other in less stressful ways. We scheduled it for the evening of Valentine's Day, 1971. Amazingly, exactly fifty men and fifty women showed up. Everyone, including me, could see that I was good at this, even inventing some new games on the spot.

So a whole new career path opened up for me. I ended up being Associate Director of Aureon, along with Carole Altman, a school psychologist and brilliant workshop leader who was the institute's program director. She and I eventually became partners in a singles organization called The Together Circle using human potential techniques and then helped found The Biofeedback Institute of New York with a scientist and inventor. I think many, if not all, of my books came out of that experience, and I definitely feel I made the most of that serendipitous opportunity. I actually first interviewed Harold Streitfeld when another prominent psychologist was taken ill. I doubt very much whether my life would have turned out as it did, if he hadn't suggested I would make a good workshop leader, or if I had been so busily engaged in other activities that I couldn't take him up on his offer.

Being open and available is a very important aspect to living a full and fulfilling life.

A Friend Creates Serendipity in My Life

This story again involves my dear friend, psychologist Rachel Harris, who introduced me to the work of Leonard Or, which got me started in the whole field of prosperity consciousness. She also introduced me to Unity Minister Sonya Milton, and came through for me again when I was still in prison and looking for a new literary agent. My former agent, Julia Coopersmith is now a bestselling author herself under several pseudonyms, and still a good friend.

Rachel suggested her agent, who sold her great book, *Twenty Minute Retreats*. Her agent was Bob Silverstein who had an illustrious career in publishing and was interested in several of my book ideas. When I was released, I sent him several book outlines, one for a book about the health effects of dark chocolate. On the phone, we discovered that we were both devotees of dark chocolate and had both discovered its delights at the Lilac Chocolate Shop in Greenwich Village in the 1970s. As we continued to speak, we realized we both lived on Hudson Street in the Village, a block apart at the same time!

Later, when I told Julia Coopersmith about this, she said she had another amazing coincidence for me. When she graduated college, her first job in publishing was working for Bob Silverstein, then head of Dell Books. Sadly, Bob passed away before selling any of my book projects. But a lot of the ideas he encouraged led to my decision to first publish this book in digital form.

When all sorts of interesting coincidences come together, I think it does mean that you are in alignment with your purpose and on the right path.

Marta

This was certainly true for another dear friend of mine, Marta Vago. Her serendipity story was told in "O", Oprah's magazine, by bestselling novelist and journalist Sara Davidson. It was about falling in love late in life and the part Marta was featured in was about falling in love again with boyfriends from the past.

It was serendipitous that I found this article online, just stumbled on it in fact, because when I was in prison I lost track of Marta, as I had of several other longtime friends, and wondered how I was going to find her. "O Magazine" found her for me with this article.

Marta was 62 when she received an email from her first love, Stephan Manes. She'd started dating him the summer she was 14, after meeting him at a piano master class in Vermont. They were a couple until she was 17 and he was 21, both students at Juilliard. Forty-six years after the end of their relationship, Stephen wrote to Marta and said he was widowed after 43 years of marriage. He was coming to Los Angeles to rehearse with his chamber music trio, and could he take her out to lunch. She invited him to her Santa Monica cottage instead and they ordered in. She did this so she could hear him play. Her piano was in the bedroom, so he played a Beethoven sonata while she sat on the bed. Marta says:

> *"It was exactly how it had been when I would visit him at his apartment near Juilliard. He would play and I would sit on the bed. In some ways it felt as if no time had passed, and in some ways I was with a stranger."*

Stephen and Marta had been apart all of their working lives. He had been performing and teaching music, and had only loved two women, Marta and his wife. She had left music, earned advanced degrees in the behavioral sciences, and had different relationships at different times in her life. In 2006, she'd been alone for five years when she visited her birthplace of Budapest, Hungary, and loved the culture and people she found there. She said to herself, *"If I'm not married or engaged by my next birthday, I'm going to retire in Budapest."* Five months after she and Stephen were reunited, they were engaged.

I have known Marta Vago since I met her and her then partner at the time when they conducted a workshop at my first Association for Humanistic Psychology conference, which I was covering for NBC Radio. I have never seen her happier than she is today.

Marta has had a lot of serendipitous events in her life, and I think it has to do with her clarity of vision, knowing who she is as a person, and following her passion in the work she does, as well as in her personal life. She also is one of the most brilliant therapists I've known and she made a valuable contribution in Book Four, **To Drown or Not Drown Stanley?**

The Value of Serendipity in Our Lives

If you are open to serendipity, you are open to finding valuable things you are not specifically looking for. Lately, I've been thinking a lot about serendipity and feeling good about having the time and space in my life to allow great things and great people in. I have the room to learn, the room to grow, the room for surprises, the room for ecstatic joy and spiritual awakening.

Robert Greene, author of *Mastery*, says that an important quality of success is to always leave yourself open to serendipity.

And former Portuguese Prime Minister, Jose Manuel Barroso says, "What people call serendipity sometimes is just having your eyes open."

I suggest that one way to explore bringing more serendipity into your life is to remember major events that didn't turn out the way you expected or desired. Was something serendipitous happening in the midst of all this, maybe something you didn't notice because you weren't looking for anything other than your specific goal? This is often the case.

Sharp focusing skills are a vital factor in creating prosperity. But at the same time you may be putting laser-like attention on something you want and missing something not a part of your goal. For example you may be focused on a relationship partner, say a specific relationship partner, and someone else much better suited for you and capable of bringing much more happiness into your life appears. If we could go back and replay a movie of our lives, we might find some very interesting things going on in the periphery of our focus area. Or some interesting people.

One more quick anecdote from my own serendipity experiences. I was at a conference and became friendly with several people there during a workshop. This was in Montreal, and this group of six or seven people decided we were going to go out and explore Montreal's Old Town. I had done a pairing exercise with a very attractive and intelligent blonde I wanted to get to know better, especially as there seemed to be some spark between us. She was walking with a man she had told me was just a longtime friend of hers. I kept trying to get her attention as we walked toward Old Town for several blocks. Nothing seemed to work. At one point, I walked up to her and asked a question. She quickly answered it and turned back to her friend.

Needless to say, I was very disappointed. It was only then that I noticed that an attractive brunette was walking alongside me, and at some point had grabbed my hand. I hadn't even felt it as I focused on the object of my original desire. I started to pay attention, and realized that this woman's hand felt very good in mine. I also found out she was also very intelligent and interesting and creative. We started a relationship that spanned several years, and we still occasionally keep in touch.

A year or so later, I did go back and look up the blonde, and we went out to dinner in New York. Nothing! A nice person, but no chemistry whatsoever. While I celebrated my good fortune in discovering my brunette, I have wondered who else might have been unnoticed at first by me, that I may not have gotten a chance to know better. And this may well be true in business as well as relationships.

We may not be able to notice or recognize every serendipitous option that shows up in our lives. We may not be alert enough to see that there is something perhaps even better than what we are looking for available to us. But I believe with some intention, we can dramatically cut down on missed opportunities and unseen possibilities. You just have to decide for yourself whether it's worth having these amazing happenings become more a part of your life.

The Word Itself

The word "serendipity" originated back in 1754 when Horace Walpole, the Earl of Oxford and the son of Great Britain's first Prime Minister, created it from a much older Persian fairy tale called **"The Three Princes of Serendip"** (an old name for Sri Lanka) These three princes had this quality, this aptitude for making desirable discoveries by accident. Walpole called it a *"silly fairy tale"* in a letter he wrote, in which the word first appears, though he evidently had coined it sometime earlier. In the letter, he described the three princes by saying: *"They were always making discoveries, by accident and sagacity, of things they were not in quest of."*

Though the fairy tale was translated from the original Persian, serendipity is officially considered one of the ten hardest English words to translate.

And with this bit of trivia, I end this chapter by suggesting you go stumble on something wonderful.

Book Seven: Building A Prosperous Spirit

"Anything you believe you are not worthy of,
you cannot have."
Reverend Ike

I don't know why, but one song, especially as sung by the late, great Nancy Lamott, and written and produced by David Friedman, just always seems to lift my spirits. And by that, I mean, I feel a surge of spiritual energy that seems to come from some higher power. Maybe I just like the tune, maybe the words themselves just resonate with me. All I know is that it's a great asset whenever I need to feel more hopeful about anything. I strongly suggest listening to Nancy Lamott singing it, which you can do by Googling: Help Is On The Way by David Friedman. I think you'll get a sense of what I'm saying, and why I feel it's an appropriate opening for this book, just by reading the lyrics:

Help Is On The Way

Lyrics by David Friedman

Don't give up the ship

Even when you feel it's sinking

And you don't know what to do

Don't give up your dream

Jerry Gillies

Even though you may be thinking

It never will come true

Life has it's own ideas of how things come about

And if you just hang in there, life is gonna work it out

Help is on the way

From places you don't know about today

From friends you may not have met

Yet

Believe me when I say

I know

Help is on the way

You don't have to know

Where the path you're on is leading

You just have to walk along

Dreaming as you go

Asking for the things you're needing

You never can go wrong

If you have faith that things are happening as they should

And just believe each step you take is leading you to

something good

Help is on the way

From places you don't know about today

From friends you may not have met

Yet

Believe me when I say

I know

Help is on the way

So open your heart, Open your mind

No matter how you've tried and failed

Tomorrow you could turn and find that

Help is on the way

From places you don't know about today

From friends you may not have met

Yet

Believe me when I say

I know

Help is on the way

Help is on the way

Help is on the way

©MIDDER Music Publishing, Inc. (ASCAP)

You also might note that lyrics such as: "If you have faith that things are happening as they should. And just believe each step you take is leading you to something good." echo many of the comments from the great spiritual prosperity teachers I interviewed for the following pages.

I have something now that I never had as a child, an imaginary friend. It's a voice inside my head that I call my Wise and Distinguished Advisor. It told me that in the interest of full disclosure, if I'm writing a chapter about prosperity and spirituality, I ought to at least mention my own beliefs. Here they are: I strongly believe in some higher power, but I don't really believe any specific or organized religion or spiritual practice has it exactly right, because I believe it was always meant to be a mystery.

It's not that I suggest any of them got it wrong, rather that any one of them may have stumbled onto the right answer, and that we really have no way of knowing. Many of my friends and colleagues have deeply held beliefs very specifically aligned with one religious affiliation or another. I don't and have received spiritual nourishment from many sources.

I have attended synagogue services (my family was Jewish, but rather secular), Catholic services, Muslim services, and various Christian services, including a holy roller church in Virginia where everyone was shouting, singing, and dancing at once, and some were even rolling around on the floor. I even once attended a snake-handling church in West Virginia, though I declined participating in the passing-of-the-snake ceremony. I have been to Wiccan events, other pagan celebrations, gatherings presided over by Eastern gurus, and many of what I consider New Thought churches. These are mostly non-denominational, and include the Church of Religious Science, Unity, Unitarian, and Quaker institutions. I got something of value from every one of them. I've also done talks at a number of New Thought churches, and even did a workshop at the Crystal Cathedral in Orange County, California. I believe an open mind and an open heart are vital in living a spiritual life. I like the motto used by Unity Church of San Francisco, "Many paths--One God."

Me and Reverend Ike

It may displease or even shock some people to know that I consider the first spiritual and prosperity teacher I knew to be Frederick J. Eikerenkoetter II, otherwise known as Reverend Ike, the flamboyant black preacher who lived a lavish lifestyle and made many millions of dollars. One reason I admired him and considered him my friend was because he was not a hypocrite, unlike many of his fellow evangelists who made a name for themselves on TV. He admitted he loved money, and said he wanted to be a role model for many poor people in his Harlem neighborhood and congregation.

He was a powerful role model, who had over two million followers in his TV ministry in the 1970s. I knew him as the outrageous pulpit performer, but also as a graceful and intelligent and spiritual and even quiet-spoken man. Few were permitted to see him in this more authentic persona. He knew what his audiences wanted and delivered it.

I first met him back in 1970, when I interviewed him for NBC Radio. About ten years later, he invited me to speak at his church, the Palace Cathedral, a former Loew's movie theater in Harlem, where he introduced me as, "The White Reverend Ike." He taught a course on **Moneylove** using my book as the text. (And if anyone out there has a set of tapes of that course, I would love to have a copy, as mine disappeared.) I once had a dinner for two with Ike prepared by his private chef in the penthouse condo he maintained in a high rise luxury building across from Lincoln Center. He was known as, "Mr. Lincoln" there.

There is nothing I can really say about him that wouldn't pale in comparison to seeing him on one of his many YouTube videos, which I strongly suggest you do. He had a big impact on the culture as well. In fact, John Lennon used a phrase he heard from Ike while channel surfing one night as the inspiration for his song, *Whatever Gets You Thru the Night.*

I had the great pleasure of meeting some of the students in Ike's prosperity class based on **Moneylove.** A number of them, under Reverend Ike's tutelage, had moved from being welfare recipients to having successful businesses, a couple had even become millionaires. I was never as impressed with Ike's collection of Rolls Royce's as I was by these humble parishioners who gave living testimony to the concept of prosperity consciousness.

We All Operate in the Same System

I like the statement David Friedman makes in the foreword to the 2nd edition of his great book, *The Thought Exchange:*

No matter how specific the method of working, no matter how "controlled" or "in the mind" it may seem, let us never forget that all that we do operates within a system that is much greater than we are and that is essentially unknowable. Call it Spirit, call it God, call it Source, I give thanks for the reliable, unswerving, omnipresence whose laws cannot fail and within which our possibilities are truly unlimited.

In interviewing people for this book, I have focused on teachers and authors who write and talk a lot about spirituality and prosperity.

In talking to three women who not only speak about prosperity, but exercise it in their lives on a daily basis, I note that they each offered some of what my friend, Barbara Winters, calls "seminars in a sentence." One example from each:

Edwene Gaines: "You have made spiritual progress when you can have your things or not, and be happy regardless."

Maggy Whitehouse: "True prosperity is a state of mind where you are radiant with health, happiness, peace, joy, and the knowledge that everything you want and need is yours for the asking."

Maria Nemeth: "A moment of discomfort is a small price to pay for enlightenment."

I don't know why it should be so, but I'm still amazed when someone who I have learned a lot from, says something new I haven't heard or even thought about before. This was true during a conversation with Edwene Gaines, a minister of Unity who always delights, instructs, and inspires her audiences at over 250 speaking engagements around the world each year.

What she said that I had to stop and make a note of and tell myself I wanted to think about later, was:

"The very fact that I have desires tells me that these desires are leading me along my spiritual, evolutionary pathway. And so I honor God when I go for these desires."

Wow! What Edwene is saying, when you get right down to it, is that we have desires because God gives them to us, and he wouldn't do that unless they were possible for us to achieve.

Imagine my surprise when just a few days after our chat, I happened to hear an interview with Archbishop Blase Cupich, of Chicago, the first American appointed archbishop, who echoes Pope Francis's call to care for the poor. What Archbishop Cupich said, which echoes what Edwene Gaines says, is:

"The aspirations that people have for a better life for their children, in which they are reaching out in hope, as many people who have come to this country have--those aspirations were placed in their heart by God. God has always called us to a better life. Has always called us to be able to provide for our families in a better way."

After that, as a prosperity teacher, I have no hesitation in telling you that you have your desires because you are <u>supposed</u> to have them, and what's more, you are <u>supposed</u> to achieve them.

A New Prosperity Perspective on The Christmas Story

One of the things that made me very successful as an interviewer on NBC and other radio venues is that I entered each interview with a sense of adventure rather than preconceived notions of what the subject was going to say. And I listened closely to what they <u>were</u> saying, so I wasn't thinking about my next question and was therefore freer to change it completely. This is still true, which is why I am often happily surprised at what the people I dialogue with have to tell me.

Maggy Whitehouse, who lives in Devon, England near Dartmoor, is a minister and comedian, but also a biblical and Kabbalah scholar. She has a different take on what probably is the most told and retold story in human history. I suppose this is to be expected from someone who can read the Bible in Greek, but here it goes:

> *I think it's interesting the thoughts we have about The Christmas Story, the one in Luke, about Joseph and Mary going to Bethlehem and there's no room for them in the Inn. If you read it very clearly and simply in the Greek, it's the most beautiful prosperity story. But everyone tells it as a story of poverty.*
>
> *It's not really an inn they go to, but an upper room in a private home., actually they probably would have been staying with relatives.*
>
> *And in those days, they had very firm purity laws. With Mary pregnant and about to give birth, she would have been kept away from Joseph in that upper room in the private home.*
>
> *Instead, they were in a stable, which would have been right next to the kitchen, so she was actually in the perfect place with lots of straw and warmth and access to hot water and where the shepherds could come visit, which they wouldn't have been able to do if Mary were in that upper room. So while this is often looked at as a poverty story, if you look at it in the social and cultural context of the time, it's not. It's a story of very beautiful, simple prosperity, which allows Mary to be with her husband and allows people to come and witness the miracle, which would have never been allowed if they followed the rules.*

Jesus was never poor, he may have been broke at times, but he was never poor--he could put his hand out and manifest anything. He just didn't want the big, complicated things that we think we want. And what we really want is peace, love, and health. and everything else is lovely, lovely icing on the cake.

Maggy on The Law of Attraction

So many people misunderstand the basic premise of The Law of Attraction, that I'd like to share what Maggy Whitehouse wrote in her book, *From Credit Crunch to Pure Prosperity:*

"The idea of the Law of Attraction has become widely known. It works on the simple principle of 'like attracts like,' or, 'Birds of a feather flock together.'

The idea of the Law of Attraction may only recently have become mainstream but it is not a new discovery. It is at the heart of the Hindu principle of karma (what you put out comes back; what goes around comes around) and it is evident throughout great religious texts including the Bible. Deuteronomy, Chapter 30, Verse 19, puts it quite succinctly: 'I call Heaven and Earth to record this day on your account, that I have set before you life and death, blessings and curses; therefore choose life, so that you and your seed may live.'

Judeo-Christian mystics have always taught what we now call The Law of Attraction as a way of understanding how life works and how to lead a happy and prosperous life; they just didn't call it by the modern name.

The Law of Attraction is immutable. It means that we attract into our lives the things that we resonate with.

All life is vibration and what you think and feel dictates the level of your personal vibration. When we feel good, we have a high vibration and when we feel bad, we have a low vibration.

It follows that if thinking about a new home, a good job or a wonderful relationship makes us feel good, then we need to maintain that level of vibration to attract what we want. Lowering our vibration with

thoughts of lack puts us out of alignment with anything that could bring us joy, and therefore it cannot show up in our experience.

Those of us who focus on love, prosperity and happiness attract exactly what we are thinking about--and those of us who worry, fret and beat ourselves up attract more reasons to become upset or dissatisfied."

There's lots more wisdom from Maggy at her website, including some videos of her comedy--she's really funny, especially when speaking about God.:

http://MaggyWhitehouse.com

For me, spirit means that part of one's experience that is not material or physical, or even mental or emotional. It is an essential part of each of us, but many people don't recognize or feed it. The word comes from spiritus or breath in Latin, certainly as essential to our life force as you can get. The word spiritual is one that also confuses a lot of people. It does not mean religious, though certainly someone following a specific religion may be said to be following a spiritual path. In America, in the years 1714 to 1818, there was a period of enlightenment inspired by a similar period in Europe. Moral philosophy replaced theology as one of the main subjects in many colleges.

The Founding Fathers, John Adams, James Madison, Benjamin Franklin and Thomas Jefferson, helped usher in this new age of reason which included the promotion of religious tolerance, and restored literature, the arts, and music as important parts of any education--something that, sadly. has often been reversed in recent years.

Jesus came up with one of the most basic rules of a prosperous spirit, *Ask and Ye Shall Receive*. This, in more recent times, has led to the idea of the Law of Attraction. As I see it, what creates a stumbling block to building a prosperous life is the separation in people's minds between the spiritual and the material. This separation is not natural, organic, or very useful.

Being a spiritual person does not mean rejecting material prosperity, and material prosperity is limited and less satisfying if one ignores one's spiritual nature.

I shared a quote of mine I posted on Facebook with Edwene Gaines:

> **"It's impossible to be spiritually or financially fulfilled if you see money as totally separate from your spiritual life."**

Edwene responded:

> *Yes, I agree with that, it's powerful. Money is a tool and yet many people worship money and they're not even realizing that they're letting money run their lives instead of spirit, and money is a convenience, it serves me and I serve God. And when you keep money in its place, it's fabulous, because we can use it to do all the good things we want to do, and help all the people we want to help and publish our books and travel, and all the wonderful things that inspire us and keep us moving along our spiritual pathway. It's simply a tool or convenience, and it's very powerful as long as we don't let it run our lives.*

Are you getting the sense that spiritual teachers have a lot to teach us about money and prosperity consciousness? I also love the lessons contained in the Zen and Sufi tales that illustrate basic life truths. One I like a lot because it gives us a chance to assess where we now are in our lives:

Become a Lake

An aging master grew tired of his apprentice's complaints. One morning, he sent him to get some salt. When the apprentice returned, the master told him to mix a handful of salt in a glass of water and then drink it.

"How does it taste?" the master asked.

"Bitter," said the apprentice.

The master chuckled and then asked the young man to take the same handful of salt and put it in the lake. The two walked in silence to the nearby lake and once the apprentice swirled his handful of salt in the water, the old man said, "Now drink from the lake."

As the water dripped down the young man's chin, the master asked, "How does it taste?"

"Fresh," remarked the apprentice.

"Do you taste the salt?" asked the master.

"No," said the young man. At this the master sat beside this serious young man, and explained softly,

"The pain of life is pure salt; no more, no less. The amount of pain in life remains exactly the same. However, the amount of bitterness we taste depends on the container we put the pain in. So when you are in pain, the only thing you can do is to enlarge your sense of things. Stop being a glass. Become a lake."

Of course, for me, this related directly to my advice for dealing with Stanley, the little negative voice in your head, that Zen teachers call "monkey mind." For years, I have suggested that people drown Stanley in a sea of positive messages. You diminish the noise, the interference in your life, and, as with the salt going in the lake, you dilute Stanley's power to harm you.

Start Paying More Attention

Many spiritual teachers advocate looking around at what's happening in the moment to see how awesome and abundant life really is. Unity minister, Sonya Milton has a very cogent comment on this:

> *I do believe when we pay attention we are in that flow of serendipity, which I call, "It Wants to Happen." And we need to <u>really</u> pay attention. It comes back to the question asked in remedial healing: Are you looking to fill up a hole in some area of your life. or are you really present in this moment to what's available?*
>
> *Because everything's available now, that kingdom's available now. And it's not always nice and sweet, but it is always rich and wonderful. For anything to happen in my life, I've got to have that energy of, 'What's alive right now?' So much is!*
>
> *My main credo is The Kingdom is Within. Whatever you want to call it, it's right here, right now. Life just gives us so many opportunities to explore that."*

MoneyLove Action Exercise

This is from an exercise I used to do in my creativity workshops, and then I found it worked well in Moneylove seminars as well. What I ask participants to do is quite simple. I tell them to close their eyes after noticing what is in their field of vision. Then I ask them to move perhaps a quarter turn in either direction, and open their eyes and notice what they may not have seen with the first look. I do this until they complete the circle. The results are often surprising to people, because we just don't pay much attention to what isn't directly in front of us. It also demonstrates that life is really about all 360 degrees of what's happening. Try it, it's one of those exercises easy to do on your own inside or outside. Of course, now with most of us always having a camera handy, you can take a picture of several different points in your turning in place, and see whether there is stuff you didn't notice before. In our increasingly busy world, we often don't simply notice what is going on around us.

More from Edwene Gaines

Edwene says the spirit of her spiritual evolution is learning to ask the right questions. She elaborated:

That's been difficult for me a lot of times because I find myself asking questions that really, I don't want to know the answer to--what I want is results, so I've learned to ask, "Tell me the next step in order to achieve the result that I'm going after." Charles Fillmore, in his book, **Prosperity***, talks about the notion that desire is the onward impulse of the ever-evolving soul. So the very fact that I have desires tells me that these desires are leading me along my spiritual evolutionary pathway.*

And, so, I honor God when I go for these desires. My question is, then, "What's my first step?" Then, "What do I do next?" And I go within a prayer and begin to ask those right questions for me. I think some of the silly questions are, "Why did this happen to me?" There's no such thing as an absolute answer to the question of "why" anything.

Years ago, one of my teachers who told me that, said, "If you have to ask a why question, at least have the good sense to make up an answer that pleases you."

It doesn't matter why. The questions I ask are, "What is mine to do and what's the first step and what's the next step and on down." Because I believe that internal guidance system is so powerful whether we're building a bridge or playing cards, or we're making a cake, or wanting to create a new friendship. To go within and ask for direction. It's right there and it's powerful.

I shared with Edwene, during our conversation, the entire contents of Book One of **Moneylove 3.0**: "Know what you want and learn how to ask for it."

Edwene:

Oh that's brilliant, that says it in a nutshell.

Jerry:

I'm sure you meet people who say to you, "But I don't know what I want."

Edwene:

And that really is actually the first step...it takes some time, to go apart awhile, away from feeding the dog, picking up the dry cleaning, washing the clothes--and go within and not ask, "What does my mama want for me? Or my spouse or my thoughts or my beliefs, but what do I really want?" And when you really are honest with yourself and tell yourself the truth, the next step is to give yourself permission to manifest it.

And not say, "Oh well, I'm too old, or I'm too fat or I'm not educated enough or I'm the wrong gender, or whatever. " But to give up

excuses and realize that your desire for whatever it is was put in your

heart by God. It's to lead you along your pathway. And then learn how to ask for it. And it's not a matter of begging God

I don't really ask others for things, When I set my goals, I go through the whole process--I visualize, I write them out clearly and specifically, And when I am asking for something from other people, I am asking for information. "Tell me how to do this."

I just learned how to Skype this past week, "Show me how to do this?" And I found that people are very willing to teach me what I need to know. It used to be hard for me to ask anyone for anything, because there was a part of me that thought, "I should know this and I'd feel stupid asking other people." You know, all that stuff that comes from that little childish ego that we drag along with us. We have to give ourselves permission to be humble enough to ask for help.

Jerry:

I like the way you have opened some workshops by saying, "This will change your life, if you are teachable." So what does someone have to do to be teachable other than just be willing to learn?

Edwene:

First of all you have to have an open mind, and you have to have discernment, because some of the things people are teaching, you might not really want to accept, but it's okay to listen and then decide for yourself what works for you.

I do believe that at some point you have to learn to give up firmly held beliefs that no longer serve you. Sometimes that's difficult and I've heard people say, "That's just the way I am." But you don't have to be that way, here's another thought--look at it this way--to begin to step outside your comfort zone. So many people that I encounter in teaching seem to be at a plateau where they can't see anything bigger than their lives and what they earn right now. And if they're content with that, that's fine, but I find they're not and they've just kind of surrendered. But if you're teachable, then you have to step up to the plate and say, "Okay, I really do believe in a loving God, I don't believe in a trickster God. And I have this desire to do whatever this thing is and so I have to have a belief in myself that I wouldn't have this desire unless it were possible."

Desires as Coming Attractions

Every desire that we have is a coming attraction, if we're willing to do our work. So, then we begin to ask, and if I'm teachable, I will allow myself to receive new information, and then I'll try it out for myself. If it works, great. If not, I just discard it and move on. You have to have a spirit of adventure, you have to have an openness to new possibilities for your life and you have to have the courage to step out of your comfort zone and do a new thing. That's what Ernest Holmes was teaching us when he said, "Change your mind and you change your life," and it's time for a lot of us to change our minds because we haven't been playing big enough.

Catherine Ponder, in one of her books, poses the thought that sometimes we have to give up the good in order to experience the greater good. So a lot of people I see are on that plateau that's not bad but it's not great. They're in survival. They're eating and they have a warm place to sleep- -their needs are met. But there's no passion or joy in their lives. And if you're not living with passion and joy, you're not really living, you're just existing. And so sometimes you have to give up that need to survive in order to get up and thrive. As I like to say, living your life in technicolor.

Jerry:

That reminds me of that great quote from my friend, Allen Klein, that: "Attitudes are the crayons that color your world." You've talked about humans having dominion over the power to name things, and that if you name something good, it will become good.

Edwene:

That's true, and to give you an example. a year and a half ago, I broke my right arm, I fell off the table at a doctor's office like an idiot. I hit the floor. I was in great pain, I literally saw stars, and I remember sitting there with tears in my eyes, saying, "I can hardly wait to see what good comes out of this." And you know, good <u>did</u> come out of it, amazing good. Because we've been given the power to speak the word, we need to be very careful so that we speak what we want to be true. Even though, in the moment, there might be pain, there might be discomfort--it might be a very hard time. There might be grief or sadness or humiliation, or whatever. If we can go apart awhile and just remember, "everything is happening for my good, whatever this is, I'm going to call it good, even if I can't see it's good right now, I'm going to call it good and because I do that, it has to turn out to be good." And I know that's true.

Jerry:

There's a song that sort of reflects that which is a favorite of mine, Accentuate the Positive.

Edwene:

I just love that song.

Jerry:

Edwene and I laughed over the pleasure of remembering the song, and it's key line,

"You've got to accentuate the positive, eliminate the negative, and don't mess with Mister In-Between."

I guess Mister In-Between describes the complacency you're talking about when you're just in a survival mode.

Edwene:

Yes, absolutely, and people just get in a place where they feel stuck and maybe they don't get any encouragement, or they don't have a model for it, I don't know what their challenge is, but I like what Wayne Dyer says, "When you change the way you look at things, the things you look at change." And you can change your life just by changing a *single thought. From, "Oh no, I could never do this, to "I can do anything."*

It's a powerful thing....even if you're not doing anything, just to start speaking those words will encourage you to get up and start doing something.

It's the gospel according to Nike: Just Do It!

All you need to do is take the first step, and then you'll know what the second step is.

Sometimes you can only see the first step taking you to your goals and desires, and you can't let that stop you. You can't be immobilized by not knowing all the steps necessary to get what you want. You need to get up and start taking that first step.

Once you do that, it becomes clearer and clearer and clearer. Nothing happens until you get up and do something about it.

Sometimes we just need to go apart and sit in the silence and let God love us as we build up the spiritual energy, the confidence, the

feelings of self-esteem and self-worth that will enable us to go out and slay the dragon, to do whatever it is that we really desire to do. It's an exciting process, but prayer comes first in my opinion.

The truth is I began my study of prosperity because I wanted to get a better life. My beginning was about getting. And now I've moved into, I still love to get, but I love to give even more. This process moved me from a scared little girl of a woman who didn't have much confidence to a woman right now where I really know that God is my source. I'm not just saying those words anymore, I know it with every cell in my body. This gives me such joy that I'm not working to get things, I'm really wanting to give back. It makes life so full of joy for me every day that I get to do this work. It's a powerful thing. I love teaching, and I know that you do, too. I know through your material and your book and all the work that you do in the world, that you're one of those people that loves to give back.

For more on Edwene and her prosperity materials:

www.ProsperityProducts.com

Dr. Maria Nemeth

Like Edwene Gaines and David Friedman, Maria Nemeth, PhD, author of **The Energy of Money**, and **Mastering Life's Energies,** is someone I always intended to have as a part of this book. I include her in this section focused on Spiritual Prosperity because I see her as a bridge between the spiritual and the world of physical reality. One reason for this is that she often works with clients who have trouble navigating the transition from metaphysical dreams and desires to manifestation in the world. Maria also often does talks and workshops at New Thought churches. And many consider her a "coach's coach" since she founded the Academy for Coaching Excellence in Sacramento, California. She got right to the point in our conversation.

Maria:

Money is an uncomfortable subject for most of us. Many people would rather talk about their sex lives than about their bank balance. We love money and we hate it. We can't live with it and we can't live without it. Money can be a source or great joy and creativity, or it can bring frustration and misery, depending on our relationship with it.

We bring all those doubts and fears, hopes and expectations, with us every time we deal with money--not just when we visit a loan officer or a financial planner, but in every area of our lives.

I want to use a very old metaphor of the pearl and the oyster. we know that an oyster gets some sand inside its shell and really gets irritated and really uncomfortable. And so it secretes this fluid which hardens and becomes a pearl. We often learn well when we're uncomfortable, when something isn't going right.

Many spiritual teachers have said that the thing that makes us most uncomfortable can be our greatest spiritual teacher if we're willing to turn and face it and learn from it.

I like to think our relationship with money is both practical and pragmatic on the one hand, and on the other hand is a spiritual relationship.

We can learn how to work with this energy--and that's what it is, it's neither right nor wrong, good or bad, it's simply energy like electricity. We can learn how to work with this energy to bring about a transformation in ourselves, and we can make the contribution we're here to make in our lives. So we don't have to be afraid of money.

For anyone reading this, the best thing to know is that you really do have what it takes to turn and face your discomforts in life.

Say we have money troubles, and we say, "Oh my heavens, I don't know if I can face it." Yet, when we turn and face it and we tell the truth and take some action--that's the key--what happens is that we find the thing that we were the most afraid of has been the agent of our personal enlightenment.

I ask our readers to think back on a time when you had a trial, something that was very hard for you and you overcame it. And looking back on it, in some interesting way you almost become glad that it happened because it did make you stronger. It helps us to transform.

Jerry

While I don't think you need adversity to become success-ful, it can often lead to success because I think it allows us to use some of those skills and talents we have that might not even come to the fore unless we're faced with a crisis and need to dip down into that reservoir.

Maria:

My definition of success over the years has been: You do-ing what you said you would do consistently, with Clarity, Focus, Ease and Grace. I ask people to look at that defini-tion for a moment and ask themselves if it would be okay to be successful with clarity, focus, ease, and grace. Maybe without the adversity and struggle.

Jerry:

One definition of grace, because you don't hear that asso-ciated with prosperity and success a lot--I looked it up, and the definition I like a lot is: Grace is elegance and beauty of movement or expression. A further definition of grace is a sense of propriety and consideration for others, and a disposition to kindness and compassion.

Maria:

Yes, grace is the inclination toward beauty of action, elegance of action, and also the inclination toward generosity of spirit and compassion. In some places, grace is also described as an unearned blessing. There's so many ways of looking at grace, it's almost like a kaleidoscope, isn't it? One of the ways that I have people begin to look at grace in their own lives is to keep track every night in a little notebook by their bed of three things for which they are grateful for that day. It could be small things, because in order to really appreciate the sense of an unearned blessing, which is not so much theological as it is just plain old spiritual-- the gateway to grace is gratitude. And learning how to be grateful for whatever is on our plate.

*It's an antidote for something in, **The Energy of Money**, I call busyholicism, which is an addiction to being busy--it's an addiction to filling our lives with so much activity that we literally don't have time to look at what's important to us. We think that "If I fill my life with a lot of activity, then I'm successful." Success and being busy are not the same thing at all. I've noticed that people who are really success- ful are not busy. They take effective and focused action, but their life isn't crammed with a lot of meaningless activi- ty. One of the things about keeping track of three things for which you are grateful is that it starts to open you up.*

*The famous writer, Willa Cather, has this wonderful quote on miracles. In her book, **Death comes to the Archbish- op**, she writes, "Miracles rest not so much upon healing power coming near us from afar, but upon our perception being made finer."*

The miracles of the church seem to me to rest not so much upon faces or voices or healing power coming suddenly near to us from afar, but upon our perceptions being made finer, so that for a moment our eyes can see and our ears can hear what is there about us always.

Moneylove Action Exercise

So perhaps this would be a good time to look at the four parts of Maria's success definition. Answer these four questions.

1. Do you think you have clarity about success and your path to get there?

2. Do you think you have the ability to sharply focus on where you are?

3. Do you feel comfortable associating success with a life of ease?

4. Do think you can learn have more grace in your dealings with money? In other words, more compassion, elegance and beauty of movement or expression?

Like most of you, I would guess we aren't completely there yet in all four aspects Maria cites. Another question: Which one of the four would you most like to improve in your life, starting immediately?

One of Maria Nemeth's prime credos is one I've adopted into my life, I have the intention of living it, and only spending time with people who demonstrate it. It's simply:

"Say what you're going to do, and then do it." A simple power-house!

Moneylove Action Exercise

This is something I often do for myself and find very nourishing and inspiriting. I sit down in a quiet place and create an equally quiet place in my head to meditate on how well I've done at saying what I'm going to do and then doing it. If this simple formula for living with integrity strikes a responding chord, realize you can make it a part of your purpose and your path instantly. And if you do, try doing these regular checkups. I sometimes make a list with two categories.

1. How well have I done recently in saying what I'm going to do, and then doing it?

2. What impact on my life recently has saying what I'm going to do and then doing it had?

I often find that life seems to run more smoothly since I began focusing attention on this practice.

And, as in everything, be prepared to forgive yourself if you don't always do it perfectly. For me, that's just a helpful message from the universe that I need to start putting some more intention and attention on it.

As I talked to Maria, I said that in her prosperity philosophy, my three core instructions for moving forward as I wrote in the original **Moneylove,** would be divided into the metaphysical, or dream and vision part of reality for a Clear Vision of What You Want and the Belief That You Can Get It, while, Putting the Beliefs Into Action would be the physical reality.

Marie:

> *One of the things for us to appreciate is that the unique opportunity in being a human being is that we have one foot in metaphysical reality which is the home of our ideas, dreams, and visions...and we have one foot in physical reality, which is the place where we take action to see results. and if we spend too much time in metaphysical reality without doing anything, we end up **"metafizzling."** And it's not a very pretty sight.*

Jerry:

> *I love that word and am only sorry I didn't invent it myself. Metafizzling is where a lot of people spend a lot of time. In fact, though I never had that great word to describe it, over the past 35 years, I have seen many raring-to-go readers and workshop attendees and audio listeners, plunge into thinking about and visualizing about prosperity, but then metafizzling when it comes to action, when it comes to creating it as a physical reality.*

Maria:

Sad but true, Jerry, because somehow we've learned that it's important to hold an intention in your mind, which it is, and it's important to be very clear about what you want, which it is, but then the missing ingredient for most of us is focused action--which you must take. To do something.

That's why going into physical reality is so important. But you see, if you go into physical reality without looking at what's important, and you just take action, and take action, and take action and if what you are going for is not really important to you, we then run the danger of being busyholics.

*Again, too much metaphysical reality is **metafizzling**, and too much physical reality is **busyholicism**, and so we want to strike a balance and thats what a lot of my work is about.*

Moneylove Action Exercise

You can probably guess what this exercise is going to be about. It's asking yourself three essential questions:

1. Can I think of a time or a project about which I had the vision of what I wanted--the dream was very clear--but I didn't take action and it metafizzled?

2. Think of a time when you weren't clear on what you wanted or where you wanted to go, and therefore ended up taking too much action.

3. Think of a time and a result where your metaphysical reality, the idea, dream, or vision, was completely in align-

ment with the focused action you took and how did that turn out for you?

Jerry:

Maria, you point out that when people are moving from metaphysical reality to physical reality, they often get stuck at the point of transfer, which you call, "Trouble at the border." And a surprising realization, you say, is that when you get to that border, you may discover you don't even want to succeed in achieving that goal or dream you had.

Marie:

*It's true. Let's say, just for the heck of it, that you decide, regarding money, that you are going to put $50 a month in a vacation savings account. Now this is very big, because what you are doing is shifting your whole relationship with money by starting this vacation savings account. One of the things i talk about in both **The Energy of Money**, and **Mastering Life's Energies**, is that life is a hologram, meaning that if you take focused action in one part of your life, it actually transforms your <u>whole</u> life.*

So even saving $50 a month in a vacation savings account when you haven't saved money for this before, it is big and it does change your whole relationship with money. At the same time, you get trouble at the border.

Let's say one of the months you are saving that $50 for your vacation, your car needs a tire, and automatically the first thought in your mind is, "I can't put that $50 in the vacation savings account, I've got to put it towards my tire." At that moment, you're at the border and the question becomes, "How can I creatively solve this problem, so that I keep putting $50 in that savings account <u>and</u> I pay for that tire with clarity, focus, ease, and grace. Not by going into more debt, but using clarity, focus, ease, and grace.

So, it puts you in a place where you have to start thinking creatively. With any project, large or small, we will always hit the border and there's a little voice inside of us that says, "Turn back, this is a bad idea, let's do the vacation fund next year. It's that little naysaying voice. I call it "Monkey Mind," the Buddhist term that stands for that part of the mind that is always chattering at us. While I like your concept of drowning out your negative voice you call Stanley with positive messages, another thing we can do is shift the focus of our attention to what it is we want to do, and learn how to do it in small, sweet steps. Monkey Mind or Stanley, is inevitable and is often a sign that you are doing something right, not something wrong. I think when we get to the border, the monkey mind tries to warn us of danger. This worked for us in prehistoric times when we needed to flee or fight, but it doesn't work so much for us now when we don't need it. But it's a sign, and if people get nothing more out of my words here, it's important to see that monkey mind is a sign that you're probably on the right path. And if you see that, in a sort of paradoxical way, you could become comfortable with your monkey mind.

Jerry:

So every time you hear that little monkey mind voice, you can say to yourself, "I must be doing something right, or it wouldn't be trying to steer me wrong."

Maria:

That's it! That's it! Really, that's it in a nutshell."

Jerry:

So, Maria, since I talk a lot about using money well when exchanging it for something you want, I am fascinated by your concept of leaking money.

Leaking Money

Maria:

Think about a bucket that has a hole in it, no matter how much you try to fill the bucket with the water faucet, with that leak the level is always going down, and the water is not even being used productively. it's just leaking through the bucket. Many of us have money leaks, and what that is is not spending money on what we really would enjoy or not spending money where it will be useful for us.

Sometimes we'll got to the market and shop, and especially when we're hungry, we'll start leaking money. We'll go to the produce section and by maybe a few extra apples than we really need, 'cause we're so hungry, or we'll got to the meat section and buy more meat than we need. The bottom line is we may end up throwing out some groceries from our refrigerator, simply because we bought too much, simply because we were hungry, and that's one of the times we start to leak money.

Leaking money could also be spending on something you buy on impulse, and you take it home, and say, "Why did I really buy this, I don't really want it!" To see if and what you are leaking, I suggest that you track every penny you spend for just seven days. The moment you spend it, cash, check, or credit cards, ask yourself the question, "Am I leaking money right now or am I spending it consciously."

One woman client of mine was leaking so much money that when she stopped, she saved so much without leaking money anymore, that she was able to have enough for a vacation at Club Med in one year. Looking at one area of your life and acting consciously, will open up all areas of your life. So when you look at leaking money, you may also see you may be leaking time, or physical vitality.

Moneylove Action Exercise

So, if you have a Moneylove Journal, as I suggested in the Instruction Manual, you can do Maria Nemeth's Leaking Money Exercise of tracking all your expenditures for one week in the journal, or otherwise just use a sheet of paper. Remember to give yourself a pat on the back for taking focused action by doing this small chore of keeping track, of doing something that perhaps you haven't done, or don't like doing. Do it.

And don't forget Maria's question to ask yourself as you are actually spending this money, "Am I leaking money right now or am I spending it consciously?" And it might be useful to ask the question after one week of keeping track, because you very well may become aware that something you thought was consciously spending has, with hindsight, turned out to have been leaking money.

Maria also talks about money as a game, and that we can imagine a playing field where we play for our goals.

Maria:

> A goal is an area or object toward which play is directed in order to score. It's looking at goals as our friends. Now, there's something else that _isn't_ a goal. It's called a task. It's like a clean-up job. Getting out of debt is a task. It's very important but it's not a goal. What doing a task does is clear your playing field so you can play for another goal. If you have not taken care of money, you might have things like seeing whether you've been balancing your checkbook. Asking yourself, "Do I have a will?" Seeing what your credit cards look like, these are not goals. These are clean-ups so I can play for my goals. You can see there is an energy difference between clean-ups, and playing for what you want as a goal you direct your play toward.

Jerry:

> *You also put a lot of attention on the concept of being willing. What exactly does being willing mean?*

Maria:

> *Are you willing?*
>
> *To be willing is your capacity to say "Yes," no matter what your monkey mind is saying. You and I can get a capacity that transcends our thoughts and feelings, our doubts and our worries. It's a capacity that comes from who we really really are. The late UN Secretary General, Dag Hammarskjold said, "For all that has been, Thank You. For all that is to come, Yes!"*
>
> *Meaning saying yes to whatever's on my journey, meaning saying yes to be fully engaged in my life. Not trying to go around something that may be an obstacle, but to be willing to look at it and see how best to proceed. You can get this tremendous capacity to say yes. So if you are meeting someone at the border between metaphysical reality and physical reality, you could say, "Do you want your goals?" And they may say, "No." But then you may say, "Are you nevertheless willing to proceed?" 99% of the time people will say "Yes!" Because they intuitively know that being willing is a reflection of who they really, and the contrast to your monkey mind is your voice of wisdom.*

If Maria's ideas resonate with you as much as they do with me, you may want to check out her website:
www.acecoachtraining.com

A Gentle Warning About Your Process

This is really something I strongly stated in the Instruction Manual at the front of this volume. There are amazingly powerful lessons throughout **Moneylove 3.0**, and that is especially true of this chapter. I call this The Density of Intensity. It's a lot to absorb all at once. If you are like one of those lookie loos, who is just skimming over the material deciding whether you want to take it in, this will be no problem. But I am assuming that most of my readers, as was true for the original **Moneylove,** consider themselves serious students of prosperity consciousness.

Pace yourself. One suggestion I have is to read one of these twelve books from start to finish first, and then decide which parts resonate most with who you are right now and where you want to go in your life. And then go back and read those parts again, slowly and with intention. And do the damn exercises!

I coined the term Information Asphyxiation to describe allowing ourselves to be overwhelmed by everything coming at us in today's 4/7 online world. Pace yourself, and to help with this, you might carefully read or re-read Book Three, **The Law of Subtraction**, which offers solutions to this information overload bombarding our brains.

I think this is particularly important with *Building a Prosperous Spirit*, because I did not err on the side of bumper sticker, talking point, sound bite sentences. I intentionally asked my fellow faculty members and contributors questions I knew would evoke detailed answers, and always had the purpose in mind that I would present their material in as full a format as possible. I think you'll agree I succeeded in doing that.

This is not a book designed for lookie loos, and I imagine any who show up won't stay long. And I trust the rest of you will be able to be your own discerning editors in which parts of the whole you take in. A number of my contributors, all of whom I personally learned some valuable stuff from, are really giving you a whole seminar on their approaches to having a more prosperous life, with more purpose, more creative fulfillment, more love and a lot more money. In fact the book itself is something I would put up against any semester at any business school in the world. But you do have to pay attention to how much you take in all at once.

On the other hand, I also include many great single sentences containing great wisdom, and in Book Eleven, **QuoteLove**, tell you how to make the most of those. That's a wide range between single sentence statements and pages of material in each book that could easily each be a valuable seminar. You may have already gotten the idea that this work is a three-tiered effort.

First, it's a volume to just read. Second, it's a collection of powerful teachings with accompanying action exercises to make it a total experience in learning. Third, it's a reference work to dip back into whenever you need to brush up on your prosperity consciousness.

A Prosperity Teacher Bites The Dust

Gee, have I stepped over the line in being irreverent about a reverend? The truth is I am bit saddened since Maggy Whitehouse told me she has stopped teaching prosperity. Maggy felt it was time to move on to her two other favorite endeavors, teaching the lessons of the Kabbalah, and doing stand-up comedy. She is making her mark in both fields, and, of course, many of her great prosperity books will continue to teach valuable lessons on the subject. And she also told me she is open to discovering something totally new that she'd enjoy doing with her life.

Truth be told, I really admire the courage it took for Maggy to make this decision, though it's one that may disappoint many of her fans. And I am happy that **Moneylove 3.0** may be the last place she offers some of her soul wisdom

about prosperity. (Though I have no doubt her own prosperity consciousness and brilliance on the subject will occasionally slip into her Kabbalah teachings and perhaps even into her comedy.)

More From Maggy Whitehouse

I think Maggy may be psychic in that I no sooner talk about

not focusing on single sentences as much as substance, than she responds to a question I asked about her feelings about prosperity with a couple of powerful single sentence declarations.

Maggy:

> **Prosperity has nothing to do with money, until the moment it has.** *And when it has, you know you have some work to do, because you've been pushing against the money for so long that you don't even know that you're doing it.* **Money's nothing as long as you know that it's nothing.** *Most people just push against and push against and don't realize they're doing it.*

Jerry:

> *I've often heard it said that money's not an issue unless it's not there.*

Maggy:

> *Yes, absolutely. And this may come out in your dislike of people who have money because you don't think they should have money.*

Moneylove Action Exercise

Can you make a list of ten people who have lots of money that you don't think deserve it?

This simple process can tell you a lot about your attitudes about money and being rich.

Maggy:

> *So many people in the spiritual world have this warped opinion that Jesus was poor and spiritual people shouldn't have money.*

Jerry:

> *I often say Jesus was really one of the greatest prosperity*

teachers in history just by virtue of his statement, "Ask and ye shall receive".

Maggy:

Well, Jesus added to that, and you can find it in the Gospels according to Luke, when he said, "Ask, believing, and ye shall receive."

Most of the prosperity issues we have are about the allowing and the receiving. So many spiritual people have this twisted mentality of toxic giving. Many of these people have their self-esteem tied up in being of use to others. They can't have a day when they are not giving to others in order to feel good about themselves. And that gets toxic and affects every aspect of your life.

I always say to people, "If you have a problem with prosperity, you've got to assume that your guardian angel, or your guide or whatever you want to call it, is like a Martian in that it doesn't actually speak your language and it doesn't know why you're doing the things you do. If it observed the thought patterns, the emotions, and your behavior, it would just give you more of what you're doing.

People will also come to me and say that another thing Jesus said was "Give and Ye Shall Receive." Well, you've got to allow the space in which to receive. If you just go on giving and giving and giving, and don't take the lazy days, don't honor the Sabbath, and don't take time to recoup, or just to sit, you're guardian or God or the Universe just assumes that you want more opportunity to give.

True prosperity is a state of mind where you are radiant with health, happiness, peace, joy and the knowledge that everything you want and need is yours for the asking

People say, "You live this amazing life." and I say, "Yes, because it's a simple life." It's a wonderful life where we take the time out to receive and allow the universe to look after us and this is the big secret, Jerry, of your concept of Creative Loafing. Its taking time out to be radiant.

That's the whole secret: to receive the radiance of God and to radiate it out.

And that is so much more powerful than just motivating people. When you motivate people, you push them and you get the monkey mind involved. At first, it's excited about all these new ideas and new plans for a short while, and then it gets bored and gets dragged down and beats itself up because that's the pattern it's used to. And you end up feeling worse than before. For some people, motivation works, but not generally for those who are of a spiritual mind and have prosperity problems.

People come to me and I ask them why they do, and they might say, "Because you radiate something." And I say, "All you have to do is learn to do that yourself."

Jerry:

One of my favorite mantras or affirmations is "People love to give me money," because I believe (or at least tell myself) I send out such an attractive energy that people will want to be around me and they'll want to partake of whatever I'm offering. I think that's the secret, whatever you're offering out in the world, your ideas, your services, your talents, your skills, your products--if you make them attractive and you present them in a loving and joyful and radiant way, people will want to exchange money for them.

Maggy:

I think The Law of Attraction, I think people kind of misunderstand it. And quite often it is misunderstood in that many people think you have to go out and help other people in order for God to aid you, when, in fact, you've got to just shine for God to be in you.

Money was invented by humanity and is a purely imaginary thing fueled by belief.

Money doesn't exist at all. Very very little money positively exists in the world. 2% of the money in the world is printed. Which means 98% of it is basically an energetic agreement between computers.

I always say, "If you're happy, if you're comfortable, there is nothing wrong, you don't have to do anything!"

But if you're out of kilter and you're not happy, then we need to work."

Money is going to come where there's passion.

If you are having trouble coming up with something you want, you probably don't really want it. You have to passionately desire it. If you have to have it, you have to have it.

Jerry:

I sort of see passionate desire as a super-fast train. You can hop on it, it's taking you in the direction you want to go, you're not steering it or running it, and so many people when they get on that train, they try to get off because it's going too fast for them. They're frightened, they don't know exactly its final destination or if it's going to get them there. But if you just relax and enjoy the ride, you'll have it.

Maggy:

It is this thing about letting go of control. The ego does not like to let go of control.

So often when you see someone and they're telling you their issues, you can see that they know what they would have to do to free themselves. The pain of staying where they are is not as great as the pain they think it would take them to change. And as soon as people know that the pain of changing is less, they immediately change.

Moneylove Action Exercise

Can you think of something that you have a passionate desire for right now? It can really impact your prosperity consciousness if you ask yourself the following questions:

1. What is my passionate desire?

2. On a scale of one to ten, how much do I believe I will get it?

3. What is standing in my way of having it right now?

4. What would I have to start putting into action immediately to be on a direct path to achieving it?

5. How willing am I to go for it, even if I have to give up some less passionate desires?

Maggy:

Abundance is our birthright and everything else is resistance.

Jerry:

So, everything that keeps us from having what we want is our resistance to it. It's not about producing a lot of money at all, it's about doing what you love and believing that you can have however much money you need when you need it for what you really want.

Maggy:

We live now in a beautiful house in Devon, on the edge of Dartmoor, and we had a beautiful five bedroom home in Birmingham before that, and people are amazed that we rent. They tell me I am wasting my money, throwing it away. I answer, "Its only money and I get it. I'm actually living in the style that is perfect and gorgeous for us, and is totally free. So if God needs me next week to go and live in Argentina, I could do it. And that to me is the hugest prosperity. Most people find that a very frightening and difficult point of view.

Most people think that owning a house is stability, but if you owe a mortgage, it's not stability at all. So I'm very happy that my prosperity consciousness has no problem renting a house, I know the money will come.

The road to joy is the road itself. Unless you are having joy now, you are never going to get to joy, because your energy in not attracting joy to you.

Gratitude is about acknowledging what you've already received, and I think one reason both the U.S. and Canada are two of the richest countries is because they both have a national day of Thanksgiving.

Prosperity is all about the feeling, about how you feel. The difficulty is that you have to start having the discipline to make sure you feel good. One obstacle is, how can you go on feeling good when the other people around you are feeling like rubbish? The answer to that comes back to the radiance again. If you feel good, the other people either have to start feeling better, or move away from you.

Some of the toxic giving energy is, "I must give of my energy to the other person so that they'll feel better. The trouble with that one is that the person can only then feel better when you are there. And they become vampires. They don't mean to do it, but they can have vampiric energy so that they eat you up. You need to be there and you need to help them in order for them to feel better, until there comes one day you are so tired you can't turn up and help them, and that's when quite often they turn around and bite you.

People have gotten into this trap of, "I feel better making you feel better and am a good person for making you feel better. But there's no radiance there. The other person can't go, "I want to be that myself." rather than "I want that person to help me." It's a simple but very very powerful difference.

When I write or talk about Biblical Law of Tithing,which is something very much misunderstood, I always say it's very simple. it's about Connect, Receive, Give in that order. And spiritual people, given it's the New Age and they're in the helping professions, tend to Give before they connect or receive. And they're always running on empty. On an airline, they tell you very clearly that if the oxygen mask drops in an emergency, put your own on first before you help anyone else, because otherwise you're going to choke to death, perhaps only getting to help one other person. Whereas if you've got your mask on, you can help as many people as possible.

You need to take the time, the Sabbath in fact, to make that connection, to sit and listen, to receive and be a part of this great radiance. To fill yourself, like the 23rd Psalm says, "My cup runneth over," so that your cup does run over, so that then you always have something to offer to the other.

You're offering it from the place of strength, from the place of "If you do this, you will be this strong." I keep repeating Connect, Receive, Give--and people have extraordinary results from just doing that. And it works for time as well as money.

The Right Order of Things

A lot of people, as soon as they get money, they pay their bills. So the Martian or Monkey Mind says, "Oh, she wants more bills" It is that simple and that's how it works.

So when the money comes in, put some toward a good experience or some workshop you want to attend, or buy some chocolate or some flowers, <u>then</u> pay the bills. It might just be ten minutes later, but you are showing the universe what your priorities are, what the order of importance is.

And you can put just fifty cents to the side to go toward that workshop you want to attend, or 50 cents toward a bottle of wine--and then maybe you have to pay $500 in bills, but if you do it in that order, you just are radiating the message, "These are my priorities."

The Peeling of the Onion

It's as if you are going up levels of the onions, you know the peeling of the onion, and you get to a certain level where you've got the prosperity sorted very nicely, and its like your spirit is saying, "Clear me out, take me higher. I want more, I'm seeking more." Then you have to add another layer, don't you?

There are rules you have to follow if you want to live a prosperous life but that's more about external prosperity, and then there are rules for inner prosperity, and the really truly prosperous life gets simpler and simpler.

I don't mean that it's simpler to <u>do,</u> sometimes it's harder to unravel those layers of the onion. but it comes down to the most incredible, simple joy, rather the havoc of having to have. We are predicated toward the physical aspects of prosperity now. But the spirit is about being open to what *is--open and accepting to what is, and that allows extraordinary prosperity.*

It really is important to get the stuff about money clear, because so many people in spiritual work have it quite messed up.

It's true that if you do your passion you will be taken care of, but so many people believe their passion is in caring for others, which means we are pandering to the ego's desire to be loved.

www.MaggyWhitehouse.com

Resilience

I've talked a lot about the importance of being resilient, being able to bounce back. It's what I did after being released from prison, and it's a quality I see in people who seem to be leading lives of total fulfillment. It's also something very much a part of spiritual teaching, and particularly in the New Thought spiritual movement. One of my dearest friends in that movement is Rev. Marla Sanderson, who was ordained as a minister with the Centers for Spiritual Living church, formerly called Science of Mind or Religious Science. She was the minister at the Clearwater, Florida church but has now chosen to create a new online entity instead of having a church.

The New Thought Global Network provides a service for those people who may not live near or want to belong to a specific congregation. It provides discussion forums, and lots of audio talks from leading New Thought speakers and teachers. Marla shared with me (and now you):

The Global Network is what I've chosen to do instead of having a church. Having a church is really demanding and isn't as much fun as I thought it would be.

I like doing the talks, I like putting stuff together, I like teaching the classes, But boy, I felt a whole lot better after I quit. It just doesn't appeal to me anymore. It's something I wanted to do for a really long time, and so I did it, and now I know it's not what I want to do now. I like to be able to travel and go places and do things.

I purposely included this very personal revelation as an example that even clergy members have that yearning for a free range or freedom-based life that some of my contributors describe in *Jobs and No Jobs*.

Marla, in the thirty-some years I've known her, has been a great model for that quality of life known as resilience. As she puts it:

What I truly, truly believe in, having been with this teaching as long as I have, is that things are always going to get better.

I also know that persistence isn't always going to get you where you want to go, if where you're going is not a good idea for you.

Life is in our corner, life is in our favor. If we know that and live as if that's so, when things come up that look like obstacles or even failures, you begin to recognize them as markers or signs along the way, pointing you this way or that. So when things seem like disappointments, they're just messages; and, you just do what you want to do, going in the direction you want to go; and, things will naturally get better.

And it's at that very moment that you have a change of consciousness, that the outer things do start to change. Because, of course, we're either the one shining that light out there into our lives, or we're not. The thing to remember is that you're always the one who's making it better, or you're the one who's making it worse.

It's always up to me, and when I clear the hurt and disappointment, or whatever is going on, it's easy to be resilient because that's the nature of life.

http://www.newthoughtglobal.org/

Well my ego is feeling pampered right now, and inspirited, which is a word I can use to describe all my contributing faculty members in this book. Inspiriting is defined as: Infusing spirit or life into someone, to enliven, to energize, to refresh, or hearten. In other words, it's like a spiritual shot in the arm. Did you feel any of this as you read the words and wisdom of my mentors and contributors?

Moneylove Action Exercise

A good way to complete this chapter, or any other chapter, is to take a moment of quiet to take a snapshot of what had the most impact on you, as of this moment right now. If you are willing, answer the following:

What one teacher, one sentence, one concept, one exercise really inspirited you the most as you read *Building a Prosperous Spirit*?

Enjoy your answer, whatever it is.

Writing this chapter has been like attending spiritual retreat about prosperity for me. If it feels the same for you, you may want to take some time and space to absorb it all before moving on to the next Book.

Book Eight: Cyber Consciousness

"Older people ask 'What is it?'" but a child asks, 'What can I do with it?'"

Steve Jobs, after giving one of the first MacIntosh computers to a nine-year-old birthday boy.

There are lots of warm-hearted, giving, compassionate people who become cold robots when they start doing business online. The idea is to warm up the Internet with human connections, not freeze it out by becoming another one of its automatons. The most successful Internet and Social Media entrepreneurs understand this.

Back in 1978, which was certainly the dark ages in terms of computers, I only knew one friend who actually had his own computer in his home. No internet, but we could see what was happening as businesses just started getting more computer-oriented. It was harder to get high quality customer service, it was harder to find a human being behind the high wall many businesses created between themselves and their customers.

I still believe there is a crying need for human contact and emotional connection. This, to me, is an essential part of what I am calling Cyber Consciousness; it's a method of navigating this new online world of opportunity in a way that is *not* about focusing primarily on the money – instead it's about knowing what your purpose is, following your passion for something, and doing it in a unique way. It's about allowing that to guide you rather than a generic sense of what you think you are 'supposed' to do in that space.

This chapter profiles those who are doing very well online-by approaching the online world in a way that's different to what many people imagine it takes to succeed. And as you will discover here, those who stand out and take off do so, not by following the marketplace, but by focusing on a deeper connection with the people they most want to reach. Which is why I picked my two current partners. They are very knowledgeable about the Internet and how to do righteous business on it, because they have hearts as well as minds, and are not afraid to reach out with emotional attractions.

Christina Makrides is a marketing and people specialist, helping small business owners with online as well as offline marketing, a good deal of which she uses Facebook for. As she says:

> *The Internet and social media play a very big part in what I do. Yet social media is highly misunderstood.*

Christina doesn't think of herself as a Social Media expert, but rather a specialist in connecting with people and creating human connections, and caring about people, as well as being a marketing entrepreneur. She explains:

> *A lot of people use social media to try to sell to their customers. And although social media is a great medium to sell, I think too many people are spending too much time trying to use it as a distribution facility, where it's all about them. "Come to me!" "Come spend money at my business!"*

> *It's me, me, me, me, me.*

> *But most people, if you ask them what they spend their time on, on Facebook for instance--what do they look at, what do they click on, what intrigues them, it's about information. They want something that's going to make them laugh, or something that's going to make them cry. They want something that's going to connect with them emotionally. People are more inclined to do research on, or click on, or open things that talk to them on an emotional level.*

> *If you're going to sell to somebody, you know, "Buy my stuff, buy my stuff," they'll just skim right by you in their newsfeed. They're not interested, they don't want to know.*

> *So that's one of the things a lot of the small business owners I work with have a problem with when they come to*

me. We start to connect with the audience, their customers, to really give them information that's of use. For instance, a restaurant can connect by highlighting their customers. If they have a birthday, wish them a Happy Birthday on Facebook and let them know they really do care and appreciate them for choosing their restaurant to spend their birthdays with.

People are looking for recognition, and they are more inclined to tell their friends, "Have you seen us on this Facebook page, come take a look."

So you're getting a lot more when you're engaging with your audience--that word itself is overused, "engaging," what does that mean? It means really caring about your customers. Without them you wouldn't exist. So instead of trying to get them to buy stuff from you all the time, it's about connecting with them and giving them things they can put into action. Or things that give them the recognition that they deserve.

Really, on a human level, caring about these people. Because once you start caring about people, they will automatically become loyal to you. Not a "Buy one, get one free," loyalty either; I'm talking about an emotional level here, where they'll come in and say, "This is my favorite restaurant, and the reason why is because I always feel at home here. I feel like I'm always taken care of when I come here."

That's what social media does for these small businesses. It gives them an opportunity to be able to connect with their customers outside of the restaurant itself, but still giving them value.

Christina's attitude about selling on Social Media reminded me of a great line from famed Internet and Social Media expert, Perry Belcher. It was in a webinar on social media, particularly Facebook. Perry said, "Immediately going on Facebook and trying to sell something is like carrying a sample case of Amway products to a party. And you need to consider that's what Facebook is, a party."

What Christina said reminded me of why I feel so good about inviting her to be my partner in creating a new brand for **Moneylove**, and starting to create much wider visibility online and in the world. As we established our very human connection, she suggested I talk to Leo Quinn, whom she called her mentor and with whom she shares a weekly mastermind Skype session. I did, and frankly, once I heard about his giving away new twenty dollar bills, being very well-versed in the world of joint-venture projects, and my friend, Barry Dunlop, told me he was a good choice, it was a done deal.

Leo provides a good reminder that true Cyber Consciousness is not just about the warm and lovely human connection--to be conscious online is also to be aware that one of the biggest benefits of the online space (the amazing opportunities to connect more widely and easily with people than ever before!) also comes with responsibility. He says,

> *I'm a great believer in the truth that you get back what you put out.*

> *And these days, when you put out something on the Internet, it's going to stay there.*

> *So I always try, particularly when dealing with things I can never take back, to put out only good stuff. I don't engage in negativity on Facebook, I don't engage in negativity on any forums, and if someone has something nasty to say about me, I pretty much just ignore it.*

> *It's impossible to hide online these days. As I said, you get back what you give out--so be careful what you give out.*

To be clear, this doesn't mean you should hide away. In fact if you want to succeed online that is simply not an option, as Leo points out! His advice for anyone wanting to do business online is:

> *Do something to stand out. Be different, be creative. I'm a big believer in what some people call "Mafia offers," in that they're impossible to say no to. Sometimes you'll see someone offering a 200% Money Back Guarantee. It shows that the person has confidence in their product. So, if you're trying to sell something online, be different.*

For more information about what Leo does, click on: www. LeoQuinn.com

Just as this online world comes with great opportunities, so this greater reach comes with responsibility. Embracing both sides is an important part of developing your own 'Cyber Consciousness', and in turn attracting the prosperity and opportunities all around us!

Speaking of which, let's turn our attention to someone who is excellent at spotting and acting on opportunities online.

Michael Dunlop

A young man who is an excellent example for anyone wanting to produce a profitable blog or online business is Michael Dunlop.

Now 55, Michael has been successfully blogging for ten years. He is now a respected veteran blogger and online entrepreneur. I have known him since he was 19 years-old, a dyslexic college dropout who started out doing something so simple that very few people have ever attempted it: Providing value without trying to sell anyone anything.

I first met Michael and discovered www.IncomeDiary. com through one of my best friends, his father, Barry Dunlop, another brilliant entrepreneur who gave me immense support in so many ways after I was released from prison, including creating my original MoneyloveBlog.com with WordPress, and getting my

38 page free online book, The *Moneylove Manifesto*, published and beautifully designed. He is still one of the people I go to for information and advice and wisdom.

Most of my contact with Barry, who lives in Surrey, England, has been via Skype and emails. But I delayed my departure for Panama by one month because he and two of his sons, Michael and Joshua, were going to be in San Francisco for a Traffic and Conversion Summit in SF--Ryan Deiss and Perry Belcher organized in January, 2013. Michael and I had already been friends for several years, but I had the pleasure of meeting Josh, another successful Internet entrepreneur and master photographer.

What impressed me most in 2009, when I was introduced to Michael by Barry, was how quiet and shy he seemed to be, despite his huge success achieved at such an early age. I was even more impressed with his business model. And how his approach epitomized prosperity consciousness (as well as what I am calling Cyber Consciousness).

Firstly, it was never about the money with Michael, though he certainly knows how to produce it and use it well. His first efforts were to provide content that would attract a large ongoing audience for his blog. He did that with such a perfect strategy that is indeed amazing that he came up with it first as a teenager:

Michael's Successful Strategy

Since he liked meeting other Internet entrepreneurs, he decided to go about meeting the best of them, and asking them to give him, the novice blogger, advice about achieving success. Then he put their answers on his blog. Word soon got out to new Internet entrepreneurs, and old hands, and bloggers and aspiring bloggers around the world, that here was a site offering the best advice possible, and it was completely free. Michael Dunlop's audience grew and grew.

Down the road as his audience grew wildly he made his first money from it by starting to share three affiliate links from Internet services he had used himself and had recommended to friends. These included GoDaddy.com, the most popular web domain site. Taking his percentage of sales generated from his readers who visited those three websites, Michael was soon up to earning $8000 a month.

But more and more kept coming, and he continued to offer great content (including an audio interview and several articles by yours truly), and his audience grew exponentially. Then he launched his Pop-Up Domination program and sold over a million dollars worth in the first year.

As I write this, Michael and his partners have launched a new website offering people access to the best Internet freelancers for a wide range of services. www.AwesomeWeb.com

Michael makes blogging look easy, and how he did it holds valuable lessons: Michael's formula was simple, provide a valuable service, truly useful information, and people will come. And that's a core theme of cyber conscious people.

It's All About Give and Take

What advice would Michael give you about entrepreneurship in a 'cyber conscious' way? Michael says:

I am in particular struck by something that I read in a survey about entrepreneurs recently:

Entrepreneurship is about solving the problems of society, not starting a business for one's own sake

And he has seen this to be true firsthand:

Before creating IncomeDiary.com, I had a few major websites--the young entrepreneurs' website: RetireAt21.com and a web design blog which I sold for over $20,000 only 6 months after starting it.

Now, it would be a bit over the top to suggest that I started IncomeDiary.com to solve the problems of society--but it

would be true to say that I started it because I wanted to solve a 'problem' — the problem of being constantly asked questions about how to create a blog or how to make money online.

It was out of solving this 'problem' that IncomeDiary.com was born. If there is one lesson in particular I would like to share it is:

That in order to RECEIVE, you must first GIVE.

I wish I could say blogging is an easy way to make money–but I can't. I can, however, say it is an excellent way to make money and frankly it does eventually become quite easy, but not until you have first given of yourself and created something of value that other people will follow.

I started this blog at the time hundreds of other make-money-online blogs started. They had all the same goal, to make a lot of money blogging. Most of them went on to earning no more than $200 and either being sold on Sitepoint or just going offline. I came to the niche with a different angle, which was to present my content in a way no other blog did.

It was really simple, I was to interview all the big internet entrepreneurs and ask them to give the advice, that way my visitors got the best advice and not just another blog post about how you can make $10 a day with Google Adsense.

The second aspect of my content was to inspire, I created top lists that would impress every reader but also give the impression they could do it themselves if they wanted to (which I believe they could).

I started out small, and I even remember getting excited when I started to make $10 a day with Google Adsense a few years ago – fortunately these days the numbers are *quite a bit higher and I even quickly started to experience some $1000 days of earnings.*

Off the back of these approaches and smart thinking, his audience has grown beyond a million visitors a year. It's gotten to the point where his father, Barry, who's been doing Internet stuff a lot longer than Michael and is also very smart, often tells me to ask Michael when I have a question about doing something online. A proud daddy indeed.

4 Tips for Cyber Conscious Thinking.

Michael says the secrets of his success are:

Providing Value

Being Inspired

Hard Work (at times)

Consistency

I have seen no better formula for online success than this. Michael says:

"We've got such a great opportunity right in front of us. This is a time where a lot of money could be made for everyone, even if you're starting today."

Moneylove Action Exercise

Here's my action exercise I think will absolutely change your life and your results:

Go to www.IncomeDiary.com and read Michael's blog posts. Pick out one that appeals to you and decide, even before reading it, that you will put one of its suggestions into immediate action if you are doing business online.

Then do it

Moneylove Action Exercise

If you are not there yet, ask yourself what you can do to create a $1000 day *every day of the week* in an online business. Make a list of three things you think you need to do to make that happen.

Moneylove Action Exercise

A four part exercise for you to do right now:

1) Check out Michael's four secrets of success and ask yourself whether you are doing all four:

Providing Value

Being Inspired

Working Hard (at times),

Being Consistent.

2) Then look at Dr. Rickie Moore's Tri-Energetics formula from Book Four, **To Drown or Not Drown Stanley**, and ask yourself where you can do more of each of these:

Know What You Need
Say What You Want
Have Clear Intentions
Be Flexible,

**Be Compassionate,
Be Curious.**

(As a side note, curiosity is not to be undervalued. Like many 'Cyber Conscious' people, Michael seems to be endlessly curious, a quality Albert Einstein says led to most of <u>his</u> successes. Michael even once interviewed me at length about my prison experience, just because he was curious about what it had been like.)

3) Now, add my three Moneylove criteria for deciding how to do your work, live your life, and use your time and money:

Do What Brings You:

**Knowledge
Pleasure
Profit**

The Lucky Thirteen

This last list of three is the kind of multitasking I approve of, when you can accomplish all three simultaneously, as Michael has definitely done in his young life. If you can do all thirteen, which I call The Lucky Thirteen, so much the better. But being human, few of us won't have a few items we still need to work on, which can make the journey even more exciting.

So if you like lists to use as awareness tools, criteria for becoming more successful and happier, and models for great business achievements, you might consider combining all 13 of the preceding items, and asking yourself whether any of them are now missing from your life and business.

Just making such a list and reading it over a few times, can be giving you more value than any MBA program at a prestigious university. If you do it, that is. Here are The Lucky Thirteen again to make sure you incorporate them into your life:

Provide Value

Be Inspired

Work Hard (at times)

Be Consistent

Know What You Need

Say What You Want

Have Clear Intentions

Be Flexible

Be Compassionate

Be Curious

Focus on what Brings You:

Knowledge

Pleasure

Profit

(And by the way, these 13 items were the criteria I used in selecting those people I would invite to contribute and do interviews for this book. Plus I'm only using those people who laughed at least three times during any interview).

4) Finally, memorize this list of 13 items so you can access it, say it silently or out loud, or write it down, as a continuing process in

your life. If you measure whatever you do or plan to do against The Lucky Thirteen, you can't go wrong.

Which is why I chose to include this as a separate action step for you: if you do it, I think I can guarantee that your life and business path will be changed forever.

The Next Step If You are Willing and Ready to Go There

For now, these thirteen will give you a good start, but if you master them, and they actually have begun to work for you, and want to go on to expand your horizons and your learning curve, you can add, from the original 1978 **Moneylove** book, the list of three things you need to do to change your life, as first offered by pioneering American psychologist, William James:

Start Immediately

Do It Flamboyantly

No Exceptions

And then you can add the three things from **Moneylove** I said were most necessary to create prosperity:

A Clear Vision of What You Want

The Belief That You Will Get It

Practical Skills to Put That Belief Into Action

Then, if you choose, after mastering and memorizing all of the above, you can add Dr. Maria Nemeth's basic mantra and rule for living well, also introduced in the preceding Book, **Building a Prosperous Spirit**.

Say What You Are Going To Do and Then Do It

And add in her four aspects of living a completely prosperous life:

Do Everything With:

Clarity

Focus

Ease

and Grace

Yes, I know there is some overlap. A clear vision of what you want is similar to Say What You Want, and Clarity, but as with any great ideas, the greater perspective you can achieve by hearing, seeing, or creating alternative ways of expressing the same idea, the more intentional you can become.

This may seem like a really ambitious formula to adopt. But remember, this is your whole life ahead of you we are looking at expanding, enhancing, prospering.

Also, most of these involve common sense, and you might take a few minutes to just think about, meditate on, reflect on, and daydream about what your life would have been like in the past ten years if you had lived by this formula, and what it might look like in the next ten years if you start using it now. And as Rickie Moore suggested for her Tri-Energetics formula, just apply any of the 25 items on this final list with some issue or challenge or obstacle facing you now.

The Complete Prosperity Formula

One repeat of the entire list, and when you get to being able to recall 25 of them fast from memory, you will be well on your path to total prosperity in all aspects of your life!

Provide Value; Be Inspired; Work Hard (at times); Be Consistent Know What You Need; Say What You Want; Have Clear Intentions Be Flexible; Be Compassionate; Be Curious

***Focus on what brings you:* Knowledge; Pleasure; Profit Start Immediately; Do It Flamboyantly; No Exceptions**

***Have:* A Clear Vision of What You Want; The Belief That You Will Get It; Practical Skills to Put That Belief Into Action**

Say What You Are Going to Do and Then Do It

***Do Everything With:* Clarity; Focus; Ease; and Grace**

I don't think I am being unrealistic or bragadocious when I say if I printed this list out on one sheet and sold it for $100, it would still be a great bargain, and all anyone would need to start making big changes for the better in their life. Right now you can get a pen and create this for yourself in a way you'll see and remember--and I encourage you to do so! I wasn't really sure where and when I was going to introduce these powerful 25 concepts from the combined wisdom of five people who spent a lot of time studying how people can be more successful. Michael Dunlop, Rickie Moore, Maria Nemeth, William James, and myself. But Michael's comment on his four criteria for success sort of triggered the idea, so I decided to leave it in this book. Truthfully, though the 25 items don't specifically refer to cyber consciousness, adopting them will definitely help someone be a more conscious person online and offline.

Big Daddy Dunlop

My dear friend, Barry Dunlop, Michael's father, shared some of his thoughts with me about what is happening now in this new age of the Internet:

> *Perhaps never in history has there been so many opportunities readily available to so many people. This is especially so for young people.*
>
> *I think there are new standards and expectations for young people-the whole idea of having to wait a certain length of time to achieve some sort of financial independence is out the window. It is conceivable to now be financially independent from a standing start at age 25 or even younger-- and at a level of wealth way beyond the previous generations' expectations.*
>
> *Also, it is also not about MONEY alone--young people today know they have choices--it is about LIFESTYLE, not exclusively about money.*
>
> *My son, Joshua, is just about to embark on some travels (with no fixed date for return) and is fully confident he can earn money as he travels and enjoy life without the ties of previous generations. This means today's Internet-savvy young people look at the world and have expectations well beyond those of their parents and/or grandparents.*
>
> *This is perhaps the greatest core change in a generation.*

To find out about Barry's latest business venture, click on: http://www.renewable-living.com/

A Cautionary Note:

The reason I titled this chapter, Cyber Consciousness, is because a lot of what goes on online is not coming from any degree of higher consciousness whatsoever. It's sometimes about hustle and hype and people lying about huge incomes to try to get you to buy something. You need to err on the side of caution when purchasing information online.

The criteria I've always liked is to get recommendations from people you know have impeccable integrity. And to only respond to a description of a program or course or book that calls out to you and touches you in some way. Get rich quick usually translates into go broke quick. And the Complete Prosperity Formula of 25 items can be used as a way to measure anyone you do business with. Very few among the many, many thousands of Internet entrepreneurs will be able to meet most of those standards. Also, good thing about online business is that it usually costs a fraction of what it cost to open an actual shop on a real street or mall out in the real world.

I am very fortunate to have people like Barry and Michael Dunlop as advisors. They both do very well in their online ventures, but are modest, authentic and rarely talk about their earnings. It takes a lot of experience to spot the fakes, which is why I consider the Dunlops my personal Santa Clauses, they know who's been naughty or nice.

A Message For My Not-So-Young Readers

If you are over 50 and reluctant to explore using Skype or Facebook, you may be missing out on a life-extending opportunity. I've had several friends tell me how uncomfortable they feel when doing something online. Part of me wants to say, *"If that's so, don't do it, after all you've survived this long without being computer literate or Internet-savvy, why change now?"* But that's not really true. Some basic skills, easily picked up at local libraries, on tutorials galore to be found on YouTube, and just by asking the kids or grandkids, can keep you out of a sort of fog where you aren't fully participating in your world.

I know the feeling, as when I came out of prison in 2008, I had never been online. So what I did was get a MacBook Pro laptop and sign up for the $99 per year One-to-One personal service. I got to sit face-to-face with a young computer expert at The Apple Store in San Francisco (and by young, I mean they were sometimes one-third my age), and ask any question I wanted to. I went at least once a week for three years, and am embarrassed to admit I had to sometimes ask the same question two or three times. The next step was and is to practice, to explore new websites and even new software. It will keep you young in many ways.

It's somewhat similar to what I've experienced moving to Panama and not speaking Spanish. There is a lot of the culture and flavor in this beautiful country and its people that I miss out on until I can at least carry on a conversation.

And in my opinion, all the research about how learning a new language keeps the brain young also applies to the language of the computer.

Know What You Are Not-So-Great At

I think it is not only useful but vital to know the things you are not great at, so you waste a lot less time trying to get better at them than focusing on what you are great at.

Frankly, I suck at technical knowledge and skill, and have been aware of this since I first tried learning how to operate the radio control board when I took my first job as a disc jockey and announcer at the age of nineteen. I could have made more money at the beginning of that career by becoming an engineer as well as on-the-air talent, especially at stations in smaller cities where they were looking for this kind of multitasking. I probably could have studied and gotten my engineer's license, but I still would have sucked at it. Instead, I learned to rely on and appreciate those who were good at it, and use their talents and information when I could.

The same is true for marketing and business logistics like bookkeeping. I resisted this truth for a lot longer as it conflicted with my inclination to be a loner. While most of my colleagues in the motivational and inspirational business had either highly competent assistants or even full staffs to handle this stuff, I did it all myself, just occasionally delegating these duties to a freelancer. What a waste of time and lost opportunities this produced! Now I have The Moneylove Team, consisting of social media expert Christina Makrides on the beautiful island of Cyprus and the brilliant Leo Quinn, who knows all about finance and setting up affiliate and joint venture deals on the Internet.

More important, to me, than their having skills I don't have, is the fact that we mesh so well in an attitude of collaboration and prosperity consciousness and having fun doing work we love.

For Everyone Over 12 Who is Not Now a Computer Whiz

If you are over the age of twelve and are not now a masterful practitioner of all the skills needed to use the Internet and Social Media easily, effectively, and productively---then don't bother--online mastery will always remain out of your grasp. Those 12-year- olds now studying advanced techniques in the field will always remain quantum leaps ahead of you. What do you do about this if it isn't your natural field of endeavor, isn't something you excel at or are passionate and exuberant about? You hire the best!

Yes, you can get someone to create a website for you at a cost of $500-$1000, and if you want to explore and experiment with being in business online. As a beginner, these are certainly plausible options. However, if you already have something of value you want to deliver and do it in a high quality way, you have two routes to go. You can hire a website designer for your business at about an annual salary of $100,000, and/or a programmer/developer, which might cost you $125,000 to $150,000 a year. These are both very good options for someone who is already established and wants to create a really large international presence online.

Or you can go to a freelance marketplace and hire the temporary services of the experts you need to get you up and running. I think the premium site just developed in 2014, by Michael Dunlop and his partner and Product Manager, Nicholas Tart, is a good option for someone who is serious about creating a successful online business. It's not cheap, it might cost you $10,000 to get a website and blog and shopping cart and all the essentials up and running, but when you compare it to starting an offline business, it's a bargain. To open a shop of almost any kind, including a franchise operation, the estimated start-up costs are $50,000 to $100,000. And that doesn't take into account hiring employees, stocking merchandise, advertising and marketing. This is why most offline businesses don't even expect to make a profit for a year or two, and many more go out of business than thrive. When comparing this big picture, paying a qualified expert a one time fee of $10,000 to create all you need to go online profitably sounds like a pretty good deal.

The premium marketplace developed to bring freelancers and clients together by Michael Dunlop and Nicholas Tart is www. AwesomeWeb.com

Nicholas Tart

I was first introduced to Nicholas Tart in January, 2013 at the big Traffic and Conversion conference in San Francisco. I was told that he was someone who was going to be a big player on the Internet. Nicholas was establishing himself as someone who was nurturing a lot of very young Internet entrepreneurs, and had a website called juniorbiz.com. He's still very interested in helping young entrepreneurs, even while being totally involved in Awesome Web, but now he is more into doing it live and in person. Nicholas told me:

> *Since we first met, I've started a youth entrepreneurship program and we're running in Ft. Collins, Denver, and Boulder, Colorado a Young Entrepreneur Tournament. So*

we take kids as young as nine years old up until 18, 19, 20, and we walk them through the process of starting a business and serving a customer. They go through the process and learn what they need to learn, and then it's up to them to go out and serve a customer.

But I mainly wanted to talk to Nicholas about this new venture with Michael Dunlop, a premium freelance marketplace. He said,

I think it's going to be very important to help shape the landscape of the internet, so my focus is on Awesome Web. We're a new company, we're small and nimble, but we have a pretty big vision for what we want to create. It's really about creating the web moving forward and making it more awesome. There are a lot of websites out there and very few of them are honestly awesome, so I think we can help with that.

Three awesomes in one short paragraph, so I imagine you can guess Nicholas Tart's favorite word nowadays. And his vision for his new company and the Internet is nothing less than awesome:

The number of websites being created isn't anywhere close to going down. If anything, the number of apps and web applications is increasing.

One of the goals is freedom of time, freedom of work, freedom of location so you have the freedom to work when you want, where you want, and how you want.

I think it's important to get started. I know that's a cliché and I know that's it's something that people hear all the time. But really, it's what's most important. You can't learn unless you're doing.

So here's a dynamic young presence on the Internet saying what I said you had to do to be successful in the 1978 **Moneylove,** "Start Immediately!" And also, of course, one of the 25 criteria on the Complete Prosperity Formula.

Nicholas and Michael have brought another partner on board, linking up with someone who already has a very successful website, another twenty-something entrepreneur, Dainis Graveris from Latvia, whose blog is in the top twenty worldwide for web designers, and who brings his web design expertise and some top freelancers to the table. http://www.1stwebdesigner.com

I think what Awesome Web is adding to the mix of freelance marketplaces out there is a level of accountability that hasn't always been present. I know a number of people who have not always had good experiences working with freelancers to get their websites up and running, or improve an existing website.

I must admit I am proud of my prescience in being one of the first people back in 1978, who said that an important factor in having successful businesses in the coming years would be to provide more human contact and connection. It seemed obvious to me then that in an increasing mechanized, computerized, and technologically advanced world, people would feel more isolated and less valued as individuals. Without exception, the highly successful practitioners of cyber consciousness I have interviewed have cited the "human connection" as increasingly valuable in the world of online entrepreneurship. Nicholas Tart is no exception :

One of the things we are doing is making the hiring process a human experience. We do that by putting up the freelancer's photos and their names because we want the hiring process to be human. So when you hire someone you actually know that person, you can read their bio and the descriptions of their projects
I think the biggest issue with integrity online is the fact that people don't know each other. As soon as you get to know

someone, you go, "Okay, this is a real person and I'm accountable to them and I'm going to do good work for them.

Michael Dunlop and Nicholas Tart and Dainis Graveris are all very experienced at creating new and exciting online entities. They all started very young and are still in their twenties. And they are definitely on a mission. As Nicholas puts it:

Our mission is to make the web more awesome, and we do that by connecting the people who do good work with the people who need good work. The way that we're different than any other freelance operation is that we cater to people who do need awesome work. On other freelance sites, you have them catering to $500 websites and people who are just getting started in business or in freelancing.

We're catering to people who have experience and a keen understanding of what they want to do online. And they always need to find people who do good work. We've had about 800 freelancers sign up and I review all their projects and portfolios, and we've turned down about 16% of the applicants. So we feature a hands-on review of the work done by our freelancers. You can't get on AwesomeWeb without being good. The nice thing about that is that these freelancers are generally more experienced than those found at any other site.

I think people need more specialized work. I think there's a lot of Word Press plug-ins, there's a lot of Word Press websites out there. And I think what people are looking for is someone who can do a very specific task, whether it's optimizing the speed, the load time of the website--or helping them developing a dynamic content within their page. I think there's a need for people who specialize in specific tasks online.

I've been a freelancer since I was 19, and I've built sites through and through. But I think as the web grows, and as there's more competition, website owners will need to put more effort into making their site unique. If you're one of tens of millions of Word Press sites, you kind of get lost in the crowd.

Now that he has established such an impressive track record, I asked Nicholas a question I am sure I am far from the first to ask. What advice does he give to someone wanting to start a career online?

To create something. In 2008, I created juniorbiz.com, and through that I got freelance clients. I started with people like Michael Dunlop.

And because I started creating something seven years ago, that's the reason I'm here today. Everything I do I can attribute to stepping out on my own in 2008 at the age of 19. And I haven't had a job in all those years either, and I've just been creating ever since.

www.AwesomeWeb.com

Even though you may not need this kind of premium freelancer marketplace (though Awesome Web calls itself a "simple freelance marketplace"), I thought it was useful to learn Nicholas's vision and his purpose for helping to create a company that intends nothing less than to change the entire online landscape. Whatever happens with Awesome Web, I have no doubt that Nicholas, Michael, and Dainis will be even bigger Internet icons than they now are. They certainly will never get lost in the crowd. This is the kind of creative energy that is so exciting and increasingly making itself felt online.

Even some experts have scoffed when I suggest that in five years, the Internet will look totally different and we will look back on 2015 as the dark ages of online business and opportunity. But I had quite a few naysayers back in 1978, when I predicted that the most successful businesses moving into the 21st Century would be those that emphasized more human contact and more customer service.

Tony Busse

One of the great things about talking to so many successful people in such a short amount of time in putting this book together, is that you can get a sense of what the most advanced thinking is in certain areas. I notice that there are certain key words most of the most successful people use. Nicholas Tart talked about two of them he is trying to help create more of, teaching people to be more specific and unique. My friend, Tony Busse, author of **Go-Mode and the End of Mediocrity,** whom I talked to for Book Ten, **Laughing All The Way**, about how he incorporates work and play into his life, also does a lot of consulting for small business entrepreneurs. And he too focuses a lot on those two trending concepts:

Advances in technology have resulted in both a lot more information being distributed as well as a large increase in the amount of people any message can reach.

Because information overload is resulting in many messages getting lost in the shuffle or people tuning out, I'm advocating the following: Pick something you are truly passionate about, something you're really into. Learn all you can about it, become an expert. Package that information and make it available at a low cost as some form of online content or a product that is easily accessible online.

Be as specific as possible, the more unique and distinct your package, the more it will stand out and be desired by those who happen to share those interests. Even better is to combine two or more of your passions.

For example, there are many thousands of hypnotherapists in the world. It would be very difficult for a standard hypnotherapist to get their product to garner a lot of attention online with the thousands of other sites saying largely the same thing. However, a hypnotherapist who also had a passion for golf and who created a package of hypnosis tools specifically to improve golfers' performance and lower their scores would set themselves apart in the industry and also benefit from having an extremely narrow target market to focus all of their attention on. Because they can now reach millions of golfers worldwide, that narrow market is more than sufficient to provide viable income.

I think this concept is very effective because it minimizes the negative effects of information overload and simultaneously makes the most of the expanded exposure that has been made available through technology.

www.GoModeTracker.com

The Three Big A's

When Tony Busse talks about finding something you are truly into and passionate about, echoing almost universal advice from successful online entrepreneurs, it occurs to me that this is usually something you also are very good at. I also have been amazed that some Internet marketers are obviously not good at all in doing what they are trying to teach others how to do. It's also about what I call The Three Big A's, which are Authenticity, Accountability, and Accessibility. Since this whole segment is about Cyber Consciousness, doing business online in a conscious way, these three qualities should be essential starting points for any online venture. Of these, I think Authenticity may be the most essential.

Look, with so much information at our fingertips, I could easily create a course on ways to optimize your LinkedIn connections. With the growth of this popular business media site, I'd have a large potential audience, and with so many new people getting involved, I could design some attractive marketing that would convince them I had the secrets to their becoming more successful using LinkedIn. And there is plenty of material I could mine, and produce a very credible product. There's one problem: I know next to nothing about LinkedIn. I'd be faking my expertise. Oh, I could learn a lot just by visiting Google, but it wouldn't really be me, and that inauthenticity would soon be very visible, as nothing stays hidden for very long on the Internet.

Since it's so easy to make up stuff and then do online searches to fill in the blanks, unfortunately many online entrepreneurs have succumb to the temptation to fake it. And it's silly, because some simple research and self-awareness can show any one of us what we are good at and what we can become passionate about sharing with an audience willing to pay for it.

Moneylove Action Exercise

If you are not immediately aware of what you are really fantastic at doing and accomplishing, you might make a list of **Things I Specifically Do Very Well Indeed.**

One way to discover what these might be is to reflect on the things in your life that people have praised you for most. Make a list of **Things I Receive a Lot of Compliments About**. It doesn't matter if it seems silly, it can still be important information for your future growth.

My items on the Compliments List would include:

"You really make complicated things simple."

"Every author or teacher you have recommended has turned out to be wonderful."

"I like your simple language and straight-forward style."

"You're the only speaker we've had back three times."

"Your double-dipped dark chocolate covered

Oreos are the best"

"You are a great hugger."

And have you noticed that the more specific a compliment paid you is, the more special and unique you feel? Well, the more your customers or clients feel that, the happier they will be to pay you lots of money for what you offer.

There's one compliment I really loved from Christina Makrides that directly led to my choosing her as a partner.

Here's the story as she told it to me:

I started reading your blog a couple of years ago. I didn't know who you were, but I soon realized that a lot of the quotes I had read online were you. And I jelled with all the information you were putting out there. So I subscribed about a year ago and started receiving your emails. I had been working on my reaching out to people, because it's a totally different world now online.

I didn't want to appear like a stalker, but at the same time, you want to be able to connect with people and let them know how they are impacting your life. And giving gratitude and thanks to those people.

So one day I got an email from you saying you were going to hand off all your products to a marketing company. My first thought was, "I hope to God whoever takes on Jerry's marketing can give the same essence, that same image, without over-commercializing it, without making it seem like everything else that's out there right now." Really, I hoped they would be able to communicate what you were all about and what the Moneylove brand was all about in a way that really connects with people.

I just felt compelled, I needed to write to you, I needed to write to let you know that I think everything you are doing is amazing. And when I looked you up on Facebook, I saw that you didn't have a Facebook page about your products. So I thought I could help. Give it a fresh look and maybe optimize it a bit. I felt I had to give you something, because of all the things I've received. So you had a surprise package you were offering of Moneylove materials where people paid a certain price for a bundle of your audios and resources--but the surprise was they didn't know what would be included! I thought, "If Jerry says this is good, I believe him." It is not in my nature to blindly give money to somebody and not knowing what you're getting for it.

That in itself says a lot about how much trust I had in you and your products and the way you've given your message out to people. So after I got the package and was amazed at how much I was getting for a really low price, I finally wrote to you. I was floored at the response I got. To be honest, I didn't expect to get a response. I'm thinking, I'm a woman sitting in Cyprus in the middle of the Mediterranean, why would he answer me? And then you answered me and I was flattered because you took the time.

Unfortunately, a lot of people these days, they're too busy preaching but they don't practice. And one of the things I love about you and about your blog is that you actually put into practice what you preach. It's very important and I think you do that effortlessly.

Well sure, I enjoy hearing such effusive compliments from a beautiful woman on a Mediterranean island, but I wanted to make a point in having Chrissie share this story. Let me first share the beginning of her fateful email:

> *"Holy Tolitos, I had no idea it would be that much content. I absolutely love your no fluff straight-to-the-point approach. Thank you for all the great work you are sharing with the world." Christina Makrides, Cyprus*

At the time I heard from her, and she offered to give me the gift of a new Facebook page, I was frustrated. Several major information marketing companies had been discussing marketing all my books and audios all over the world for the past several years. One in particular was always telling me they were excited about bringing me aboard. They would say they'd absolutely get back to me in a week, and two months would go by with no word. This happened with several organizations.

Meanwhile, my decision was more and more definite. I wanted to be free to create content and not spend time marketing or on the logistics of doing business. I decided if I didn't have something happen in this regard by the end of 2014, I would give up on the whole Moneylove franchise, and focus on writing and also on my aspiration to be the first English-language stand-up comedian in Panama. It, for me, was another illustration of the powerful truth that what you want comes to you a lot faster when give up your attachment to it happening.

So, doing a Skype call with Chrissie Makrides, I found out she was very savvy about Facebook and marketing online, and I thought to myself, "How can I persuade this woman in Cyprus to take over all my marketing?"

Well, it turns out that while she was happily working with small businesses on her island, which has suffered great economic distress in the past two years, she felt she had the knowledge to play on a much bigger stage, and this would give her a great opportunity to do that.

So many things could have prevented this from happening, that I think it can be considered a serendipity moment.

I only decided to do my surprise package as I was tired of waiting to hear back from the marketing company. I only responded to Chrissie's email because her subject line, Holy Tolitos, got my attention. I only thought of asking if she would take Moneylove on after she offered me the gift of creating a new Facebook page. And it all felt right, including the addition of Leo to our team.

Moneylove Action Exercise

Who would you like to reach out to who has inspired or stimulated or taught you something of value? And what do you have to offer that person in your appreciation of what they do in the world, as well as being grateful for any lesson you learned from them? (Don't pick me, that would be too easy.)

Write an email to that person, and you don't even have to send it unless it feels right after you are done. I can't promise your efforts will be rewarded with a new career opportunity like Chrissie has, but if you do send it, it will be appreciated.

Remember that at this point in time people are easier to reach than ever before! Some thought leaders and authors, of course, have gatekeepers to keep too many fans from contacting them, but don't let that dissuade you. You have to start trusting the universe will deliver anyone who is right for you to be connected to in ways you may not now imagine.

Connecting With People On a Personal Level

As you can see in the example I shared above, the internet has opened up the opportunities for discovering and communicating with people. However it's important to remember that real connections are about the personal, not the mechanical.

As I already have mentioned, for many years I've talked about this, even before the Internet came along, and it's even more of an issue now---we're getting so mechanical in our connections to other people. Personal contact is greatly diminished. People are texting each other or emailing without remembering there's a real person on the other end. Chrissie Makrides proved the value of reaching out in a human way, as has Michael Dunlop and Nicholas Tart. I talked some years ago in Moneylove Seminars about one way to become more successful, if you want to create some new business models, is to produce more ways of giving people more personal attention and participation.

Though it's something he is not given much credit for along with his other world-shaking accomplishments, Steve Jobs demonstrated how important this is. When he created the Apple Store a lot of people thought it was a crazy risk. A number of analysts and publications predicted the stores would be a huge failure. Steve Jobs created the first one in 2001 in Fairfax, Virginia, and now they are the leading retail chain by far in the U.S. There are 4 of them in 16 countries.

At the time they began, people were saying the retail business, where people go into a store and buy things, is dead, that everybody's going to want to buy online--it's faster, it's easier, it's more convenient. So what did Steve Jobs do in spite of this widely held opinion?

He created The Apple Store, where people had personal contact with computer experts--with the Genius Bar, with the One-to-One service, which allowed a complete technological idiot like me to go in every week and spend an hour, one-to-one and face-to-face, with a computer expert ready to answer all my questions...for a total of $99 a year...what an amazing bargain! With free classes going on day and night on various aspects of computers, iPhones iPads and iPods. And the stores are filled with people, morning noon and night.

The New York Times said that this turned boring computer stores into sleek playrooms filled with gadgets. This proves that when you give people a good reason to interact with other people, they're going to take advantage of it, and when you give them a feeling that they're important and they're getting individual attention you can't help but be a big winner.

Martin Boroson puts it very well, *"The more virtual we get, the more hungry we'll be for real contact, real experiences that are meaningful."*

My next contributor easily feeds the hunger Martin mentions with meaningful and real experiences and very real contact even when she is doing it via Skype.

The Cantwell Connection

Originally from Australia, Marianne Cantwell's official base these days is London--but the truth is she has made the *world* her home as well as her oyster. Beautiful and brilliant, this 33-year-old travels the world, making a living online with her laptop.

She has created a whole new movement since her entry into the online business world over five years ago. The movement is called Free Range Humans, and Marianne literally wrote the book on it: **Be A Free Range Human** was one of the UK's bestselling new entrepreneurship books of the year--showing the thirst among so many people for this way of thinking.

And it's my humble opinion after talking to many successful Internet entrepreneurs that this down-to-earth woman doesn't begin to grasp how far ahead of the curve she really is.

From time to time during our Skype interview, Marianne would tilt her head and look up as if she was tapping into some higher knowledge most of us aren't even aware exists. On the following pages I will share some of these insights with you.

As has been my habit and intention in this book, I will not edit her comments, which I think constitute a powerful seminar on the world of online business. And I will only interrupt her flow to ask a question, or highlight something that leaps out at me as profound.

Being Yourself Online

Talk about bringing more of a human connection to Internet commerce, Marianne Cantwell is a powerful demonstration of the wisdom of doing this. Even though she has many thousands of people all over the world reading her free blog, and makes plenty of money with her online courses and mentorships, she isn't about money or just teaching people how to make it online.

I asked her, "So, you basically are teaching people how to create a business that supports their passions and the kind of life they want to have? Her answer clarifies her role in the world:

Marianne:

I teach people how to get paid to be themselves.

If someone's considering doing an online business, or has one already but it's stalling, the best question to ask is who you want to be. If you go into this saying, "What I want to be is someone who makes lots of passive income thanks very much," and you don't actually know what you want to do or who you want to be or who you want to help--well I've never seen someone go and be successful in that way.

But if you go and say, "This is what I want to do in the world, this is who I want to be in the world," and then add, "Hey, I can do a version of that online," -- those people tend to do better financially and in terms of their impact as well.

There's so much hype about online business these days that it masks how simple and human it can be when you take it back to first principles.

I don't think of myself as an online business owner. I think of myself as a free range human, as self-employed, and as an entrepreneur. The fact that my business happens to be online is the same as saying "I have a red shop" or "I have a shop in an alleyway."

So ask what do you want to do in the world, and who do you want to be in the world - and now let's put that online. It's not alien: it's as difficult or easy as doing an offline business, just with a different format.

As an aside: I agree with Marianne that the distinctions between on and offline are often more blurred than people imagine, and you may increase your opportunities (and enjoyment!) by getting 'conscious' about the ways to cross between the online and offline worlds.

For example I find it interesting that both Christina and Leo (profiled earlier in this chapter) not only work a lot online, but also do business face-to-face in their own neighborhoods. Leo does that in and around his home in Ballston Spa, New York, not far from the famed Saratoga racetrack, while Christina plies her trade in Cyprus. Therefore, they both get to do people-to-people business with at least a portion of their clients. This fits in well with me, as I do the same when I go somewhere to do a workshop or seminar, or when I do a Skype coaching session.

Getting Paid to Be You

Marianne:

I think teaching people how to get paid to be themselves is subtly different from getting paid to do what you love. Because what you love changes. With me, it changes day-to-day, month-to-month, year- to-year.

But once you know what it means to be paid to be you, that's powerful then you can then show up in the world and step into your best role no matter what you're doing!

For example, someone could say today, "I want to help people with prosperity or money consciousness." And let's say that particular person's natural flow is as the writer or creator of that information, and their innate style when they aren't trying to be someone else is say, very down to earth. But what if they don't know that, or know that that style and format is more than ok?

Well, without this awareness, they are entirely likely to look at someone else who has a live workshop model, and who is quite fluffy in their style--they might look at that person who is different from them, but happens to be in the field they want to succeed in and say,"Oh that way of being is what it takes to be successful." Then they try to mold themselves into being someone they are not. That's when things start to go wrong!

Carbon Copies Rarely Succeed

I see this all the time, people come in and say, "I want to be a coach," or, "I help people out with their websites, and I need more clients." And then they think, "Maybe I need to see who's successful in that field and be like them."

Now, about ten percent of those people will luck out because they really are like the successful person they're looking at.

But everyone else will be moving away from their flow and becoming carbon copies. All the while becoming ashamed of who they are, and hiding that more and more. And that's where the online world has moved lately: we have lots of carbon copies instead of people who are successful in their own right for their own reasons.

That's partly why people can get frustrated --If you are told the only way to get where you want to be is to copy this other person's model instead of identifying and real-

ly stepping into your own flow, then you end up acting at less than half your capability and experiencing a lot of frustration! Without this realization you may not understand where that comes from.

Knowing Your Own Value

Interestingly enough, the super successful online entrepreneurs I talked to for this chapter all had one thing in common, they talked about the importance of bringing value to the marketplace. Marianne got to the heart of this by saying:

Marianne:

To me, the most important thing you can do is to know your value in the world. And the way you learn that is by doing projects--little, low- to-no investment projects, that I call 'Free Range Projects'.

And the power of the Internet, which is why I'm such an online advocate, is that you can do this and have a reach out to people that we never had before. If I had been doing what I am now doing just a short time ago, I wouldn't have had the reach I have and the impact I have in such a short timeframe. I wouldn't have been able to start a blog, get readers that for some reason liked my quirky, strange style, and made all the other noise out there. And that to me is why online is a great platform, a great format that we're so lucky to have right now.

But Isn't It Crowded Online?

People will sometimes say, "But it's a very competitive field, there's too much noise out there." And when it comes to the online world, yes there is a lot of noise out there, especially in the past few years.

There's a lot of noise out there, but put that in context: it's noise in space that didn't even exist before. Go back ten years and where it was then. We didn't even have this platform then! Don't forget that in terms of opportunity we've gone forwards, not backwards.

Also, consider that your biggest competitors (or, as I prefer to call them, 'comparitors') might be helping you more than hindering you--others who are more established in your space have created the need, created the awareness for this sort of offering. That's huge. Because of them some people are already thinking about it, potential clients have already been in that headspace meaning they are even more likely to buy.

Even if you only get a third of the number of customers that Big Established Person gets, it's quite possible that they and others like them created those customers for you.

The online world is giving us more opportunities than there have ever been before. A great question to ask is, "How can I use this place that is now thriving to do what I want to do in the world?"

Manual for Living and Being

It used to be that you'd start a business because you wanted to do something you loved doing and/or you had something you wanted to bring to the world, or you wanted more financial or time freedom.

However, lately, I am seeing more and more people getting sucked into comparisons and pressure to be someone or something that takes them away from what they wanted in the first place.

So, I see people reading the success stories and seeing someone's pictures and comparing their insides to that other person's outsides-or as I say, compare your warts and all reality to someone else's success reel.

For example I know people who feel pressured to smoothly build a seven figure business from Day One --which is crazy, as when you look under the surface, no one does things that way!

This topic could be a whole other book in itself, but it's why I love that you're talking about Cyber Consciousness here:

We have this amazing platform, and amazing opportunities, so many possibilities.

We just need a manual for being and living in this online world.

Meaning and Attraction

The real key to online success is creating meaning and creating attraction--or more specifically, marrying the two.

If you have someone who is good at creating attraction, but they have no interest in creating meaning, then you have emptiness. While if you have someone who creates meaning but doesn't know how to create attraction, then you'll see a lot of frustration and lost possibility.

(That's when you get people saying, "No one pays for that sort of thing" or "I put it out there and no one was interested," even while people around them are loving their work.)

I think what the Internet is doing and will continue to do is show people who want to create meaning how to have that attraction, and link up people good at creating attraction with opportunities to create meaning.

Jerry:

I thought this last point was a vital one, so I asked Marianne to elaborate on exactly what she means by "attraction."

Marianne:

> *Simply you have something (or someone), and people and resources, or even money, are led toward it, like it's magnetic. You have an idea and people gather around it. You have an event that you're putting on and people want to be in on it, even before they know exactly what it's going to be. And that's very powerful. Once you have attraction, you have a lot you can do in the world.*

> *Many people who want to get started in the online world tell me they want to create meaning. I say to them, "that's great, and if you want to create meaning, you've got to create attraction as well." Because if you don't have attraction, then your meaning exists in a void. But if you have attraction without meaning then what you have will be empty.*

A Seminar In Itself

You probably already realize that you have just experienced a very personal and very powerful seminar presentation from Marianne Cantwell. As she was talking, her face alight with excitement as she shared her enthusiasm for these ideas, a new term popped into my head, which certainly describes her, Cyber Charisma.

Most people are first attracted to Marianne and her website and blog because they know or have been told about the fact that she earns a solid income while being self-employed and traveling around the world.

When they get to know her better, they realize she's really about something more human. What Marianne teaches is as simple as she says:

"I teach people how to get paid for being themselves."

As she explained to me, knowing how to be yourself (in a very exposed world where there are many pulls to be more like someone else) is an important part of Cyber Consciousness

:

Now that I've said that, you'll see more and more that those who really stand out do it by being themselves, not trying to be more like someone else!

Marianne's lifestyle is a reflection of this. We did our video chat while she was relaxing in Sydney, Australia, one of her regular ports of call, and I was in Panama. She had just come from Costa Rica, and I wouldn't be surprised if her next stop was Bali, another regular destination, as is the island of Mauritius, off the coast of Africa.

When I first approached her, I had been told that she traveled to a different country every month. But that's a more frenetic lifestyle than the one she actually enjoys and has repeated annually for several years. It's a sort of annual migratory circuit she makes, and she prefers spending two to three months in a place. These places often include London, the U.S., her native Australia, Bali and Mauritius. Her recent visit to Costa Rica and Peru for a few weeks was her first visit to Latin America.

And as the laptop community extends (and she visits family around the world) she emphasizes that the more you do this the more you realize how normal it is becoming; often choosing her destination based on the people she wants to spend time with, she isn't just throwing a dart at the map and letting that decide her destination.

What Life on Your Terms REALLY Means

Marianne told me she often gets asked by people how they can create location independence in their lives, and many people have asked her to teach location independence. But Marianne Cantwell refuses to do that as her main thing because she says:

It's very very simple. You learn how to do online business... and then you buy a plane ticket. There's pretty much nothing else I can say about it!

For more information on Marianne, her book, and her blog and other services, click on www.Free-Range-Humans.com

I'm not going to comment on what Marianne has told us in this generous outpouring of valuable information, tempered by her wisdom and experience of dramatic online success. As you have just seen, she speaks for herself very well indeed. But as I was listening, several exercises to try out some of her thoughts and concepts occurred to me. So here we go:

Moneylove Action Exercise

The first thing you should know before starting an online business really involves a lot of what I am calling Cyber Consciousness.

Take some paper or write in your journal. Now read the three questions below and come up with as many different answers as seems right for the following questions:

1. **What do I want to do in the world?**

2. **Who do I want to be in the world?**

3. **Why do I think this belongs online?**

(Go through these as many times as you like to build up the answers--Marianne's tip is to not to self edit, instead write down the first thoughts that pop in your head. Then when you're done put the pen down and go through them in a leisurely way, getting curious about the patterns in what you've written--and whether any stand out for you!)

You can also get a little help from your friends. Get someone to sit down with you (it can even be a Skype call) and your task is to repeat as many times as possible, "What I want to do in the world is_____" Your partner's job is to listen to each new completed sentence from you and say, "I believe you." That's all, no further comments.

And when you have done this with as many repetitions as feels comfortable (well, maybe a few more), stop and discuss between you whether the other person really did believe you, and which thing you filled in the blank with they thought was the most true, the most possible, the most authentic thing of all you said.

Your job now is to repeat the other two obvious questions by saying, "In the world, I want to be_____, " and "I think this belongs online because_____." Your exercise partner is just there to give you the automatic response, "I believe you." And to discuss which answers felt most right to his or her ears. Ask yourself which ones seemed most real for you.

Moneylove Action Exercise

Assuming you don't want to just be a carbon copy, and if you don't know of one already, start studying some people who are where you think you might like to be. Find someone whose story or approach you admire, but more importantly someone with whom you have some traits and attributes in common!

Remember Marianne's admonition to not become just another online copycat. You will find writing down, All The Things I Have In Common with _____ a useful way to move forward.

As a bonus challenge, you can attempt to make contact with this person, to ask them for advice, to give them something first, such as why you appreciate what they are doing and offering. We live in an era when it is much easier to get in touch with just about everyone directly. Explore that possibility and you might just be surprised--just remember that a few people not responding is just part of the game, so keep going and you might just get an unexpected boost!

Moneylove Action Exercise

This exercise is aimed at finding out whether you can come up with some little, small, fun "Free Range Project" as Marianne described it, to learn or test out your value in the world.

Remember, one of the big advantages the Internet gives you is its wide-ranging reach, as Marianne says in her book, a bigger reach than ever before possible in human history. You can therefore test a lot of small samples of what you want to offer to a select audience, before taking the plunge into doing it really big.

Just ask yourself, "What are one or two small projects I can easily create and try out?"

Even if the folks in your interpersonal environment have given you little encouragement or positive response to your ideas, remember they are only a small segment of the population, and may not even be able to offer an objective opinion if they know you. Trying things out with people you don't know as well can be even more valuable and useful.

Moneylove Action Exercise

Finally, make an effort to figure out what is most attractive about you.

Even if you think you know the answer to this right off the top of your head, there is probably more about you that is attractive than you realize.

This is something it is worth taking a week or so to explore in your own mind. Memory can play an important part in this process. Think about what you have said or done in your life that has drawn the most positive attention from others, gathering them toward you almost as if you were magnetic. Write out the things people have praised you for, or asked you for, in the past. If you have a relationship partner, ask them to help out by answering the question, "What would you most like to get or learn from me?"

As if often the case, people in your life now probably know more about what makes you attractive than you do. And if they don't, you should probably start hanging out with new people.

Book Nine: Jobs and No Jobs

"We're here to put a dent in the universe.
Otherwise, why else even be here?"
Steve Jobs

We can get a sense of how rapidly the world has changed by the fact that someone who had such an impact on it died at a relatively young age, and yet accomplished more in his 56 years than many visionaries do in much more time, and perhaps lived four or five lifetimes in his span. I'm talking of course about Steve Jobs who sat astride the computer age as a colossus in his own right. There is hardly a person alive today who isn't influenced by what he did, who hasn't benefited from his extraordinary grasp of the future and what would be needed to navigate it successfully. He not only thought outside the box, he created his own box, and then got everyone else to peek inside it, and often buy what they saw therein.

But what I think Steve Jobs represents that hardly anyone else has commented on, was the dramatic transformation of a society of mostly salaried white collar and blue collar employees to a society of no collar entrepreneurs.

Steve Jobs never had a job. Oh, he may have occasionally had an executive above him on paper, but even then he was usually the majority owner of every company he was ever involved in. And through his making the computer available to so many individuals, he created the technology and the space for them to also become the joyfully jobless (a phrase coined by my friend Barbara Winter, whom we'll hear from a lot in the next section of this Book).

Many of us are living our lives today according to an instruction manual written by Steve Jobs. I like to study billionaires, and think many of them have a lot to teach us about success. However, when it comes to prosperity consciousness and all its aspects of a life well lived, I haven't found any who match Steve

Jobs in their understanding of what it's really all about. Perhaps his year in a Zen Buddhist ashram prepared him in a special way for the impact he would have on the world.

While I consider Jobs the shining light inspiring people to choose entrepreneurship over having a job, he did not talk much about this. I imagine he didn't want to upset the more than 50,000 employees of Apple, Inc. worldwide. However, he did what he didn't talk about. Many former Apple employees have set up their own businesses, mainly in the tech area, thanks in part to the extensive training and education available to each Apple employee. The average employee at Apple headquarters in Cupertino earns over $125,000 annually. And there are lots of other perks on the two Apple campuses, lots of recreational activities.

The company usually goes after young innovative graduates. I've talked at length with a couple of dozen employees at The Apple Store in San Francisco over a period of four years while I visited the store for my weekly one-to-one consultation. A number of them have already started small companies on their own, and a number dream of designing an app that Apple will eventually buy, while others are taking courses in fields that will help them become entrepreneurs in the not-too-distant future. I would suspect that Apple will inspire more future entrepreneurs with their own start-up companies than any other tech company. I think Steve Jobs would smile at that. Maybe we should posthumously change his name to Steve No Jobs.

The official Jobs biographer, Walter Isaacson, is someone I admire a lot, even before that book was released shortly after Jobs' death in 2011. But in one area I disagree with Isaacson, who says Jobs revolutionized six industries: personal computers; phones; music; animated movies; tablet computing, and digital publishing. Not even counting that he was largely responsible for the shift from a manufacturing and service economy to an information and digital economy, Steve Jobs has almost singlehandedly delayed what was considered the death throes of the retail store in 2001, just before he opened the first Apple Store.

And without Jobs, the new trend of the laptop entrepreneur would not be possible. He also inspired people doing creative work at home by moving the computer world from one in which most computers were in business offices, to where the personal computer took over, and this also helped trigger the dramatic expansion of the Internet and social media.

There's not much more I can say about Steve Jobs that hasn't been already said. But there's a lot he said that could be a roadmap for being more successful in life and in the work we choose.

How You Can Learn What Steve Jobs Knew

Steve Jobs famously said, "I would trade all my technology for an afternoon with Socrates."

I would trade everything I have studied and learned about entrepreneurship for an afternoon with Steve Jobs. I actually consider that more valuable than an MBA from Wharton, Harvard, or Stanford. But you don't have to give up anything because he left his legacy behind in the form of many quotes and interviews in which he generously shared the philosophy and specific approaches that created his biggest successes.

Steve Jobs let his mind run free, without ordinary restrictions, limitations, or judgements--he was a one man brainstorming session. I suspect that the world will continue to be astonished at some of his products still yet to appear for years to come. This is why I like his quotes so much, they often address aspects of life in new ways, in ways that I haven't thought of before, in ways that take my own mind off in new directions.

Jobs liked to tell the story of how as a 12-year-old, he read an article in Scientific American that told of a test of movement efficiency among different species on the planet, how efficient in terms of burning calories each species was. The condor won the top spot, while humans came in about a third of the way down the list. But in what Steve Jobs called a brilliant stretch of the imagination, one of the researchers decided to test the movement efficiency in getting from point A to point B of a human on a bicycle--and it blew the condor out of the water. Jobs went on to say that we humans are tool builders, and here is where he came up with the phrase that struck me as profound on many levels. saying:

> *That's what a computer is to me: the computer is the most remarkable tool that we've ever come up with. It's the equivalent of a bicycle for our minds. We can fashion tools that amplify these inherent abilities that we have to spectacular magnitudes.*

What a great simple concept that places the computer in its most effective and useful role, as a device or tool for increasing the movement efficiency of the human brain.

I see this as illustrating the amazing adaptability of the human mind, the power of our ingenuity to solve any problem, or make up for any deficiency by sheer creative mental power, by using our imaginations, but also choosing and even designing and building the tools we need along the way.

This book puts a lot of emphasis on doing, rather than just thinking about doing. (Do the damn exercises!) Steve Jobs agreed:

> *The doers are the major thinkers. The people that create the things that change the world are both the thinker and doer in one person. Leonardo Da Vinci was not only an artist, but also mixed his own paints. He knew about chemistry and pigments, and human anatomy, and combining all of these skills. The art, the science, the thinking, the doing is what produced his exceptional results.*

And of course, anyone who has read Moneylove, and the longest chapter in that book, titled Worklove, will know why the following Steve Jobs quote strikes a particular responding chord in me. He said,

The only way to do great work is to love what you do. If you haven't found it yet, keep looking. Don't settle. As with all matters of the heart, you'll know when you find it. And, like any great relationship, it just gets better and better as the years roll on. So keep looking until you find it. Don't settle.

This could have been Steve Jobs' mission statement... think about the power contained in these six sentences:

"The only way to do great work is to love what you do."

"If you haven't found it yet, keep looking."

"Don't settle."

"As with all matters of the heart, you'll know when you find it."

"And like any great relationship, it just gets better and better as the years roll on."

"So keep looking until you find it, don't settle."

Most of us have found ourselves settling at one time or another..but from all that I've read about his personal and work history, Steve Jobs never did. There's a role model to build our dreams on!

And something for each of us to look at in our own lives.... is there anything in your life right now you are settling for? Maybe we all should put that sign on a wall we see every day...or as a sticker on our mirror...or a screensaver on our computer....**Don't Settle**. What would change in your life, if you really got to see that at a deep level of awareness on a daily basis:

DON'T SETTLE!

Moneylove Action Exercise

It may make you uncomfortable, but it would be a good way to clear some stagnant stuff out of your consciousness. Ask yourself:

"As I look back over my life, can I list five things I have settled for?" As you write them down, also describe your feelings about what that settling felt like at the time you made the decision to do it. And what it feels like now.

Perhaps the most important question to ask yourself:

"Do I have the capacity and courage and emotional strength to refuse to settle from now on."

Picture how that would present itself in your life, and how you think it would impact your future results.

Barbara Winter, invented the idea of a "seminar in a sentence." Steve Jobs was very good at creating a seminar in a paragraph. One of his best:

"Your time is limited, so don't waste it living someone else's life. Don't be trapped by dogma — which is living with the results of other people's thinking. Don't let the noise of others' opinions drown out your own inner voice. And most important, have the courage to follow your heart and intuition. They somehow already know what you truly want to become. Everything else is secondary."

On Your Own Without a Job

Like so many women I've talked to, who did not like a job they were in, Stephanie Donegan quit her job in 2009 with no plan or strategy for the next step in her life. Within three months, she was evicted, her car repossessed and had a total of $21 to her name. She told me this as she was having an extended vacation in Bali.

So I hit rock bottom and at the time I was a single mom with a two-year-old. I was reminded of something I had promised, that I would not allow the circumstance of being a single mother prevent me from providing everything that I desired to provide for my child.

I started trying to find what I was good at and what I could find to generate some income. So I got involved with a beauty product I had been recommending and I decided I was going to sell this product. I used some of the marketing skills I had learned and developed in my corporate job to focus on bringing this product to market. We were very successful launching this new beauty product and we got a lot of media coverage. With this exposure, people started reaching out to me, and asking how I did it, so I began sharing with people how they could successfully market their business. I also realized that this beauty company was not where I want to be long term.

So thats how I ended up in the marketing industry, and in three years it's catapulted me into a seven figure annual income.

Right now, with my eight year old son and my assistant, I am on a one year trek around the world. And in doing this, I'm really showcasing that you can create your life, you have complete control over it, you can manifest the things that you desire

Stephanie Donegan offers programs costing up to $70,000 a year which involve clients getting a lot of hands-on time with her, and even meeting her in exotic luxury destinations around the world to participate in small group training sessions. She explained that, of course, these are people who already have achieved a level of business success and want to move on to the next level. And they are more business owners than entrepreneurs. They're people who may be already making $100,000 to $300,000 a year, and she says they can double that by learning the structures and strategies of producing multiple strains of income.

Now here's something I noticed, not only about Stephanie Donegan, but about many women out in the world of self-improvement seminars and coaching, as well as online marketing--they are high energy, charismatic, sometimes in-your-face personalities, and different styles appeal to different clients and customers. But, and this is very, very important for you to note, the Internet is so vast, the customer and client base so limitless, that any strong presence will attract people willing to pay money to learn what they perceive you already have. One thing that Stephanie emphasizes is that in order to be successful and earn seven figures, it has to be layered marketing. So she offers individual digital programs, one day intensives, and many other products. She also enjoys working with people who are not ready to make a $30,000 to $70,000 annual investment for her services.

As an African-American single mother who hasn't had a job since 2009, Stephanie appeals mostly to women who want a piece of the dream. And she delivers that so that they keep coming back for more. I say women, because that is her largest market, women around the world, along with a few brave men.

I have personally noticed that men are often more timid than women when creating an online presence, or they are more stuck in the way business was done before the digital age. Women have definitely benefited from what was originally a negative experience, that they were not welcomed into the business community with open arms, so many girls did not study for business, and therefore were not stuck in old paradigms when the world dramatically shifted.

I cannot tell you how many millionaire women entrepreneurs have told me they were successful because they didn't know they weren't supposed to do what they did to become successful.

I remember a great book title from a real marketing genius, speaker Pam Lontos, whose first book was titled, **Don't Tell Me its Impossible Until After I've Already Done It.** Pam was a protégé of Zig Ziglar's. I once spent a day on Rodeo Drive in Beverly Hills with Pam, watching her work her magic, and utilizing something I dubbed The Assumptive Attitude. It's an attitude that says, "I know you are going to say yes to me, so I will keep going until I get that yes." My friends Wayne Dyer and Mark Victor Hansen have that assumptive attitude as well. To varying degrees, most of my women collaborators and contributors for **Moneylove 3.0** have it. It is a forward movement energy that is hard to resist.

I asked Stephanie Donegan, "What is your one piece of advice for someone who is in a job and would like to not be in a job?"

> *The first thing I would say is that they have to become very clear about what it is that they don't like about being in that job. Many people who leave a job because they don't like being in that job, they leave and start their own business and create the exact same thing that they did not like in their job.*

> *So you really need to be clear on what you don't like, and really clear on what you do want.*

You've probably noticed that there is a major overlap between Book Eight, Cyber Consciousness, and this section, which is one of the reasons I put them next to each other in **Moneylove 3.0.**

Because the Internet is such a dominant force in everyone's life and business efforts today, there was often a decision to make on which book to place which interview in. But I invite you to just realize that if you want to earn a good living while not being an employee, the Internet is going to have to be a part of your plan. As Stephanie Donegan put it:

> *Even if a client is in an offline business when we start working together, by the time we finish, they are going to have an online presence. We are in the digital age and it's not going to go away anytime soon, and it's going to multiply and be the way that someone can create an international*

global company, to reach the people in China, the people in Australia, etc.

You may have noticed as you read **Moneylove 3.0,** something else that is different about it. Most of my contributors are women. For a book being written by a man, this is quite unheard of. And it was not really intentional--I went for the best contributors on these subjects, the people who inspired and motivated and mentored me. More and more, these are women. I asked Stephanie about this.

There does seem to be a trend of more and more women going online, being successful, and not having to do it the old-fashioned 'old boys club' way. She responded:

Women are really stepping into their power, they're realizing their power. Historically women have been caretakers of the home. We have been taught to sacrifice our wants, our needs, and desires in order to take care of home and take care of family.

Now, we're in a time where women no longer have to make a choice between, "Am I going to be a wonderful wife and a wonderful mother, or can I have this successful business?" This is because of the use of the Internet, and because of the use of all these wonderful software programs.

Women now have the ability to get out, to serve on a higher level, to make really great money <u>and</u> be the wife and mother that we desire to be. We're not at that place where it's no longer a choice, you can have it all.

Some people who come to me and see my lifestyle, traveling around the world, think that's what they have to do, and give up the stability of home and family. And what I'm always telling people is "We all have different seasons, and right now my season is travel. But for you, a freedom-based life and location independence may mean it's your time to be at home with your family, to be there when the kids come home from school." 'Freedom-based' means I don't have to get up until nine o'clock if I don't want to. I don't have to get up at 5 am and put on a suit and stockings and go into work. I can keep on my pajamas, and i can go into my office and grab my laptop and work.

The big mistake a lot of people make is looking at other people to discover what freedom-based means. But you have to decide, because freedom means something different to everyone. And it doesn't necessarily mean travel. It might just mean I have the freedom to make my own decisions.

http://StephanieDonegan.com

My next two guest stars (really, I should say Superstars!) for this subject have inspired and taught thousands of people to become successfully self-employed, thus greatly contributing to one of the hottest trends in recent history. The trend toward living your passion and realizing you can't really do that as well with a job as without one. Barbara Winter has been a friend and mentor, and before that she was a student, first in one of my early 1980s writing classes at The Santa Barbara Writers Conference (where else would I meet Barbara the writer?) and sometime later as a participant in one of my Moneylove Seminars in Boulder,

Colorado. To tell the truth, though she looked vaguely familiar, when I interviewed her in 2012 for my Moneylove Club audio series, I didn't remember either of those instances until she told me about them.

Barbara epitomizes one of the great satisfactions for me in teaching, mentoring, or writing. When the student takes your information, makes it her own, and then becomes your teacher as well. Her book, **Making a Living Without a Job** directly led to my knowing this topic had to be a part of this book and she had to be a major part of this segment.

One way she contributed before I even started the book was by introducing me to her friend and colleague, Marianne Cantwell, author of **Be a Free Range Human**. Marianne teaches people, as she puts it, *"To get paid to be themselves."* Which she elaborated at length about in the preceding Book 8, **Cyber Consciousness**.

Neither Barbara nor Marianne consider themselves evangelists for self-employment, but rather as resources for those who are thinking about taking that courageous step away from a job, or business, that doesn't fulfill them. In fact, Barbara says:

> *I would never be an evangelist for this kind of thing if you have to bring people in kicking and screaming, they're not going to be very successful. But through a process of self-analysis, people start thinking, "Well, what if I just starting doing something on my own..."*

> *So many people have been freed from a life of conformity and boredom by what's going on, that there are some tremendous opportunities for anyone who wakes up and says...."Wait a minute, what's the next chapter of my life going to be about?"*

Marianne Cantwell on the Freedom to Choose

It seems to me Barbara and Marianne are talking much more about freedom and self actualization than about self-employment or starting your own business. As Marianne puts it:

> *There's such freedom around us, and yet we're having these conversations as if there's not. People are going around saying, "It's so tough." Well, yes; its not as if you can wave a magic wand, but it's easier than its ever been. I think the biggest thing at the moment is being aware of the freedom that you have, and that freedom for many people might involve having a job. I have no problem with that.*

Telling Your Story

We all have stories to tell, and I've always felt they contain vital information about who we are and what we offer to others. I have found it true that people who have started their own businesses usually have the most interesting stories, whereas people who have jobs have sort of stopped their story before it really got going. In this book, I share a lot of my story, and I notice that Barbara Winter and Marianne Cantwell are equally comfortable sharing theirs. It helps to know where someone comes from, especially if you are considering seeking their advice or using them as an inspiration or role model. More of Marianne's story:

> When I started my business, I never intended to teach people how to make money or how to start a business. That never was what I thought I was going to do in the world. When I left my job, I started out helping people get jobs, which is ironic, I started helping people do their resumé and have a better interview. A business I had before Free Range Humans was ironically enough about helping other people get different jobs! But the biggest question I got asked when people would come to me for career coaching was, "How did you quit your job?" So I started to blog about that, and that's where Free Range Humans was born.
>
> I started helping people figure out what they wanted to do as their own boss and thought that would be that. But once they'd done that, people would come to me and ask, "Ok, so how do I make that into an income? And I would say "Well, it's very easy, you just charge people for it." But funnily enough, they wanted more on the 'how', so after a while I started teaching that.
>
> Every step I've taken has come out of need from other people and me wanting to fill that need. I never said that I want to be known for helping people with their businesses. In fact I started out with a commitment that if I ever think

that what I do shouldn't exist anymore, if people don't need this help anymore, or if online businesses stop being a good option, I won't do it anymore. There are always other possibilities out there!

There are always going to be very sensible reasons to not leave your job, or to not leave a business that you don't enjoy. But what we miss is that there may be even better reasons to start your own thing.

Not The Reasons Why Not

If you want to do anything that's outside your comfort zone, the single best tip I've got is to look for the reasons <u>why</u> something might be possible, instead of clinging onto the reasons why not.

If you talk to people who are consummate critics, constantly saying "Things can never change", You'll find that they will be waiting for that moment when they find out that the person they are hearing about who did that thing they insist is unfeasible, was a bit different from them. And then they pounce, "Aha! They had a house, so they could quit their job because they already had shelter." and someone else might say, "Aha! They don't have kids, so they could do it." Or, "Oh, they already had a family, so they were already set up so they could do it."

I've been in the center of this. I've heard <u>every</u> reason why not. And as in those examples they're often polar opposite to each other! The very thing someone thinks they are missing, someone else has it and cites it as a reason they can't do something (a good/bad salary is a common example. Youth/experience of age is another).

Your task, if you're doing anything you're considering quitting or dropping is to get serious. Instead of looking at all the reasons why this might be a bad idea, get a piece of paper and make it a practice for a solid month to look for the reasons why it might be a good idea. Number one, the first place to look is in your own reasons, "Why would I want to do this." And ask, "How could this go well as opposed to how it could go badly?"

Number two: Look at people who have done it. Sit down for 30 minutes-- get names of people, people you don't know, people you do know. Then look at how they did it and look at the similarities with your situation. Not the differences and not the fact that they had a different education, not the fact that they live on the other side of the world. Just a simple question: what are your similarities, just start pulling them out. That practice is very powerful.

It may show you some things you have that you've been totally unaware you have on your side up to now. And it's also going to reset the balance away from the bias toward staying in a job--or in anything that's not right for you right now. Actually, the biggest thing you come up against is that we're not going into this as a balanced thing. "I'm going to go through the options in a balanced way" is a myth unless you do this. The thing is, the scales are tipped towards you staying in a job, because that is what everyone around you has done!

So to get to a true place of making a balanced decision, you have to go back and weight it the other way--you have to weight the reasons why. You have to find more of those sorts of free range people to hang out with. You have to spend time with people who think that not having a job and making a salary is normal, is absolutely a normal thing to do and is more than possible. Start spending time and you begin weighting back, and once you've weighted back, then you can make a balanced decision, then you could say, "Wow, look at all this evidence, now let me look at all my options, now let me make a better decision." When you do that you'll have so much more clarity.

Jobs As an Option

Reading the above, one can see that Marianne Cantwell avoided the trap that many new entrepreneurs, or people trying to find out what to do in the world run into. She didn't <u>just</u> sit and try to see where her life was going for years on end or making lists of options, yes she explored that but also ventured out into the marketplace to explore some of her original ideas about the services she could perform. And <u>then,</u> and this is a very important **And Then...,** Marianne paid attention to what the marketplace wanted her to do, how people out in the world want to use her and what they wanted to learn from her. She very naturally evolved into the Free Range Human she is now, creating a whole tribe of fellow Free Range Humans around the world in the process.

But she points out that she is not anti-job, she just wants to even the playing field:

> *I have plenty of friends who have jobs and they're very nice people! But there is an assumption that jobs are the right choice for 90% of the population. And that simply is not true. There are a lot of people who don't fit that model.*
>
> *It's not about saying, "Scrap the job!" I think that's an awful approach --some people might be better off in jobs, some people are much happier with that structure. But to assume that we all should want to do that, or that most of us do, or that a job is the only practical option, is absolutely wrong. I think where the future of jobs actually lies is in it being an option equal to self-employment, equal to having a franchise equal to whatever else, and that will enable you to look at and see your options much more clearly--whereas right now it certainly isn't equal.*

Getting Personal With Barbara Winter

Barbara told me this story as an illustration of the situation many people find themselves in and that both she and Marianne have helped many people figure out.

I have a sister who worked in an office in her home for many years for a large publishing company. And I visited her at her office many times and when I saw her there, she was just stoic, sitting at her computer. Put a power tool in her hand, and her whole body language changed.

And I think so many people never get that power tool in their hand. When she was remodeling a house she just bought, she just was having a great time, while it sounded like agony to me.

I think we have an obligation to find out what sets us on fire.

I think we have an obligation to take responsibility even for the quality of every day--not just the big stuff, but the little stuff, too.

Causing Our Creative Spirit to Slip

One of the things that hasn't been discussed very much in our culture is how going into what we've been told we're supposed to go into causes our creative spirit to slip. So sometimes it's really hard to access it again. It's like a muscle that just hasn't been used. We don't trust it, we don't trust our own creative ideas.

Barbara talks about why being self-employed can be a better path for someone with a creative mind and a large vision of where they want to be.

Don't you find when it's work that's part of a bigger picture it changes your attitude? Something that if you were just doing it in a job you would think it was dreadful. But when you're doing it for something that really matters to you, it's just part of the whole journey.

I'm surprised at some of the things I do that if I had a job where I had to do stuff like that, I would say, "Oh, this is the worst," but it's different when you're doing it for your own goals.

Moneylove Action Exercise

If you have had the experience of having a job and also had the experience of working for yourself, answer the following question.

"Which of those two work experiences felt more like you were being yourself and utilizing more of your skills and talents in doing it?
"

Perhaps the biggest change in the human experience is the fact that we now consider passion and loving what you do as a vital factor in our work. Only the very few and the very, very talented had this opportunity in previous generations.

One sharp example in my own life occurred during my broadcasting career. Compared to most jobs, that was a wonderful experience. I never worked a forty hour week, was paid well, and go to do all sorts of interesting and fun things. But then someone suggested that since I had collected a lot of my own and other people's bloopers, mistakes made on the air, or while recording a commercial, that I might put together a talk on this subject, and intersperse it with some of the bloopers. So I did it.

My first engagement ever as a public speaker for a business organization paid me $50, not very much. But I loved doing it! And it planted the seed that led me to quit broadcasting altogether a few years later and start writing books, and doing talks and workshops. I still fondly remember the blooper that got the biggest laugh in that talk. It was me with a terrible case of hiccups during a public service announcement done live on the air. I think it was for handicapped children, and every few seconds a very loud hiccup emerged.

The hiccup even had a burp in the middle of it a few times, and came so suddenly, so without warning, that I could never hit my cough button in time. It only went on for a minute, but it seemed like an hour. And at the end of it, I looked out the studio window into the newsroom and saw many of my colleagues laughing hysterically, which in turn started my own laughing jag. It was a horrible but horribly funny few minutes on live radio, which was fortunately being recorded by the engineer. And the highlight of the event that led to my being self-employed at 32 and forevermore.

I talked a lot in my book, **Friends**: *The Power and Potential of The Company You Keep,* about the importance of surrounding yourself with a supportive interpersonal environment that was in synch with your highest goals and potential. As Marianne did, Barbara talked about this powerful resource.

> *Start hanging out with people who are making a living without a job and you'll find its very contagious.*

> *You know I love quotes and one of my favorites is by the Persian Sufi poet, Hafiz:*

> *If your heart cannot find a joyful work*
> *The jaws of this world*
> *Will probably*
> *Grab hold of your*
> *Sweet Ass.*

The Media Gets It Wrong Again

In one of the many examples of how badly informed we are by today's news media, every time new employment rates are announced, after giving us the good news, the broadcaster will turn solemn and say something like, *"But we also need to report that many people have left the work force and are no longer looking for work."*

This is depicted as bad news, a tragedy. There is no doubt that in some of those situations, the person has just given up, frustrated by not being able to find a job. But I strongly suspect that many of those people have stopped looking because they would rather do work they love and follow their own dreams instead of someone else's.

When it comes to telling you how to make the transition from having a job to being on your own and growing from there, I consider myself a general practitioner while Marianne Cantwell and Barbara Winter are specialists. So rather than saying any more on this subject, I will refer you to them. They each have very readable and very successful blogs on the subject, which are free.

To find out more about Barbara:
www.JoyfullyJobless.com
And about Marianne:
www.Free-Range-Humans.com

There is no doubt that some people are absolutely preconditioned and predetermined to find their passion within a job, with its safe structure and someone else calling most of the shots. However, I also believe that the confines of a job and the life of conformity and rigid timeframe that usually embodies keep many potential creators and innovators from ever creating great works, great products, great new services, great new companies.

We return to the words of the entrepreneurial master for a final thought on the subject about what it takes to be successful when starting any new venture or adventure in life. Steve Jobs said:

"There's a phrase in Buddhism, 'Beginner's mind.' It's wonderful to have a beginner's mind."

Editor's Note: (End)

Editor's Note: *We hope you›ve enjoyed Volume Two of Moneylove 3.0 and that you've gotten great results from the various exercises listed within. Please join us for Volume Three which will includes the final 3 Books of Moneylove 3.0. In this Volume Jerry covers additional fascinating topics and offers more of his unique and highly effective exercises. Here is a quick preview:*

Book Ten *Laughing All the Way--Inspired by a quote from Og Mandino, this book looks at how valuable humor can be, and how important having fun making money can be in creating total prosperity.*

Book Eleven *QuoteLove--You may have thought you loved quotes and gained a lot of wisdom from them, but you ain't seen nothing yet! The introduction of Jerry's powerful new tool, Quotercises, designed to exponentially increase the impact your favorite quotes have on your life, momentum, and fulfillment. There's 100 of these little exercises, so this book can provide years of positive experiences just by itself.*

Book Twelve *Weapons of Mass Distraction--Another exclusive Moneylove 3.0 creation, this final book contains seven of the most effective strategies for becoming happier, more prosperous, and a lot more fun.*

Additional Resources:

We are very pleased to continue Jerry's policy of always giving people more than their money's worth, as such we've got two great offers for you.

By using the link below you will receive a Free Audio of Part 1 of Jerry's iconic Money Love Audio series

http://www.gomodetracker.com/moneylovefreeoffer

In Addition...

The same link will also contain the following exclusive offer related to the Go-Mode Success Tracker mentioned several times in Moneylove 3.0:

A FREE Copy of the book "Go-Mode the End of Mediocrity" as well as close to 50% off of the amazing Go-Mode Success Tracker accountability tool.

NOTES:

Printed in Great Britain
by Amazon

45333611R00093